AGE, CAPITAL AND DEMOCRACY

AGE, CAPITAL AND DEMOCRACY:

MEMBER PARTICIPATION IN PENSION SCHEME MANAGEMENT

TOM SCHULLER

Gower

© Tom Schuller 1986

All rights reserved. No part of this publication may be reproduced, stored in a retrieval system, or transmitted in any form or by any means, electronic, mechanical, photocopying, recording or otherwise without the prior permission of Gower Publishing Company Limited.

Published by
Gower Publishing Company Limited
Gower House
Croft Road
Aldershot
Hants GU11 3HR
England

and

Gower Publishing Company
Old Post Road
Brookfield
Vermont 05036
U.S.A.

Schuller, Tom
   Age, capital and democracy: member participation in pension scheme management
   1. Pension trusts—Great Britain
   2. Management—Great Britain—Employee participation
   I. Title
   331.25'2   HD7105.45.G7

Library of Congress Cataloging-in-Publication Data

Schuller, Tom.
   Age, capital and democracy
   Bibliography: p.

   Includes Index
   1. Pension trusts—management. 2. Pension trusts—investment.
   I. Title
   HD7105.4.S38   1986   332.6'7254   85-24950
   ISBN: 0 566 009285

Printed in Great Britain at the
University Press, Cambridge

Contents

	Page
List of figures	vi
List of tables	vii
Acknowledgements	viii
List of Abbreviations	ix
Age, Capital and Democracy	1
From Gratuity to Deferred Pay	23
The Extension of Collective Bargaining	37
Economic Democracy: Member Representation on Trustee Boards	55
Controlling Owners	80
The Impact of Member Representation	107
Strategic Participation and Social Contracts	139
Appendix: The Glasgow Research	154
References	157
Indexes	165

List of Figures

5.1 Lines of influence running to and from pension funds in their position as owners of equity capital   89
6.1 Does the size of pension funds affect their responsibilities as investors?   125

List of Tables

1.1	Persons aged 60 or more at census dates	7
1.2	Civilian labour force economic activity rates 1971–1983	8
1.3	Total pension fund holdings, 1978–1983	13
1.4	Distribution of UK shareholdings by market value	13
2.1	Numbers of employees in pension schemes	26
4.1	1979 Government Actuary survey on numbers of schemes and of members according to whether a representative of employees is a trustee	69
4.2	The participation profile of trustee boards	71
4.3	Date of introduction of member trustees	73
5.1	Leading fund managers, 1984	96
5.2	Ownership and control of listed UK equities, 1980	98
6.1	Rankings of trustee activities	108
6.2	Do trustee boards ratify or initiate decisions?	110
6.3	Contribution of member trustees to trustee board activities	111
6.4	Availability of information	118
6.5	Perceived key agents in trustee functions	121
6.6	Training received by member trustees	134
6.7	Most common source of advice for member trustees	135

Acknowledgements

Not only acknowledgements but thanks to:
The Leverhulme Trust, for financial support; all the respondents and interviewees for their time; Jeff Hyman for his collaboration and Laurie Hunter for his advice during the original research; Jean MacAskill for deciphering the manuscript and Jessica Gould for managing the revisions; and Stuart Burchell, Leslie Hannah, Jeff Hyman, Richard Minns, Mike Reddin, Jim Tomlinson and (especially) Sue Ward for their comments on the text at various stages.

Abbreviations

APEX	Association of Professional, Executive, Clerical and Computer Staff
ASTMS	Association of Scientific, Technical and Managerial Staffs
BIM	British Institute of Management
BIFU	Banking, Insurance and Finance Union
BSC	British Steel Corporation
CBI	Confederation of British Industry
CIR	Commission for Industrial Relations
DHSS	Department of Health and Social Security
EEC	European Economic Community
EETPU	Electrical, Electronic, Telecommunications and Plumbing Union
EIRIS	Ethical Investment Research and Information Service
ETUI	European Trade Union Institute
GAD	Government Actuary's Department
GMWU	General and Municipal Workers Union (now GMBATU after merger with Boilermakers' union)
IDE	Industrial Democracy in Europe
IDS	Incomes Data Services
IRRR	Industrial Relations Review and Report
NAPF	National Association of Pension Funds
NCB	National Coal Board
NUM	National Union of Mineworkers
OECD	Organisation for Economic Co-operation and Development
OPB	Occupational Pensions Board
SERPS	State earnings-related pension scheme
TGWU	Transport and General Workers Union
TUC	Trades Union Congress
USDAW	Union of Shop, Distributive and Allied Workers

1 Age, Capital and Democracy

A decade or so ago the American management guru Peter Drucker wrote a long article entitled 'Pension fund "socialism"'. In it he argued that:

> ... if 'socialism' is defined as 'ownership of the means of production by workers' – and this is the orthodox definition – then the United States is the most 'socialist' country in the world. Through their pension funds, employees of American business own today at least 25% of equity capital of American business. The pension funds of the self-employed, of public employees, and of school and college teachers own at least another 10% more [sic], giving the workers of America ownership of more than one third of the equity capital of American business. Within another 10 years the pension funds inevitably will increase their holdings and will, by 1985 at the latest, own at least 50% of the equity capital of American business. (1976, p. 1).

1985 has passed and Drucker's predictions have not been fulfilled. But in both the US and the UK, which have similar occupational pension systems, pension fund assets had by 1985 reached enormous proportions: about $900 billion and £140 billion respectively. ('Billion' will be used throughout as 'thousand million'.) In the UK they had by 1983 already clearly overtaken individual investors as the largest single category of shareholders, with 29 per cent of all shares quoted on the Stock Exchange. Moreover, in many cases — and especially in the larger funds which each amount to several billion pounds – employees, as members of the scheme, are represented on the trustee boards which have formal authority over the disposition of these funds. Quite often the representation is on a parity basis, with as many trustees elected or appointed by the members of the scheme as by the company. If we take only four of the biggest public sector funds, the Post Office, British Telecom, British Rail and the National Coal Board, employees have equal representation at board level in the management of schemes with assets totalling about £20 billion, by most standards enough to secure a controlling stake in a good many of the top hundred companies. Does this mean that we are living in an economy that has not only been 'socialised', but is also under workers' control?

Clearly not. Drucker's argument is both hyperbolic and based on a very jejune notion of socialism, as the inverted commas in the title of his article partly acknowledge. Yet he identified an issue of major economic and social significance. On both sides of the Atlantic the sheer size of their assets is generating interest in, and confusion about, the power of pension funds in a modern corporate economy. But this is not the only reason for the awakening of public interest; there are at least three distinct strands to the debate, each of which has considerable significance in its own right.

The growth of the funds themselves is one, from relatively insignificant bodies quietly and almost exclusively tied up in government securities to huge institutions which own large chunks of shares, great swathes of the countryside and a sizeable proportion of the national debt. Secondly, employment, health and population trends have led to major changes in the age at which people finish work and to an upsurge in the numbers of elderly people needing and deserving financial support. Occupational pension schemes figure prominently in the patterns of obligation and dependence which characterise the relationship between pensioners and the rest of society. Thirdly, we are at a period in the chequered history of industrial democracy when the participation of employees in the management of pension schemes is arguably one of the more significant recent developments, at a time when representation of the interests of labour is generally on the defensive.

These three strands are all to do with management: the management of capital; the management of age; and the degree of democracy in the management of the schemes. Yet they are evidently very disparate, and it is this disparateness which accentuates the political and administrative problems involved. Each strand is tied to a different set of objectives and involves different problems and expertise. Broadly speaking the first is concerned with the behaviour of a large segment of British capital, including its general impact on the jobs and prospects of the labour force as a whole; the second with benefit levels and the equitable treatment of people who have left the labour force; and the third with the right of working people to take part in decisions governing their working – and subsequent – lives. There are very varying ideas on the relative priority to be accorded to these different objectives, as well as on the best means of achieving them. And there is room for serious doubt about how far they are actually reconcilable. Available management skills – economic, social and political – rarely span all three.

This book focuses primarily on the third of these strands: employee participation in the management of pensions. It addresses itself to the following questions: what are the prime forms of employee participation in pensions decision-making? what are their origins and why have they emerged in the way they have? what sorts of tension between different interests has this involved? what impact has it had? and what factors shape the degree of influence that employee representatives have been able to exercise? Underlying these specific questions is a more general theme, namely that the control of the capital involved and of the benefits which flow from them is an issue of mounting significance which cuts across social and economic policies at both national and corporate levels. It brings together matters of immediate importance to individuals and strategic issues which reach well into the next century, fundamental to the distribution of wealth and power with all the attendant strains and conflicts that that implies. If this sounds rather portentous, it is nevertheless clear that pensions are a benefit which has come in from the fringe.

In this introductory chapter I shall take up each of the three strands and give them more substance. Chapter 2 contains a summary account of the evolution of occupational pension schemes, focussing particularly on the implications for the relationship between employer and employees. Chapter 3 builds on the acknowledgement of pensions as deferred pay and therefore as subject to a similar kind of joint regulation as are other forms of remuneration. It develops the theme of industrial democracy, pointing also to significant peculiarities about pensions negotiations which mark them out from orthodox bargaining. This and substantial other parts of the book are based on empirical research carried out in collaboration with Jeff Hyman at Glasgow University and described in the Appendix. The rest of the book focusses chiefly on participation in the boards of trustees which are formally responsible for the funds. Chapter 4 sets participation at this level in the more general context of 'economic democracy', as new forms of ownership and patterns of control emerge in companies and other organisations. It describes the functions of the trustee, and charts and explains the growth in the incidence of member trustees, that is those who are on the board as representatives of the members of the pension scheme and not as representatives of the scheme's or the organisation's management. Chapter 5 moves on to the role of pension funds as major repositories of capital. It reviews the long-running debate on the relationship between ownership and control, which has moved into a new phase with the emergence of giant financial institutions. It provides a simple guide to the way in which different agents are involved in the control of the funds, as well as to the influence of the funds on companies in which they have shareholdings. Chapter 6 addresses itself directly to the effect of member trustees, showing that their influence over the disposition of the funds as capital is limited and presenting a number of reasons for this. It examines other aspects of scheme management where participation has had a more significant impact, notably the dissemination of information. Chapter 7 contains some reflections on parallels between two forms of board level participation: member trustees and worker directors. It concludes with a discussion of three types of contract involved in the management of schemes: between society and its older members; between the managers of capital and those whose welfare depends on its effective use; and between the members of the scheme and those who represent them in its management. Each contract concerns one of the strands identified at the beginning.

The book is concerned with occupational, or company, pension schemes, not with pensions as a whole. Occupational pension schemes are 'agreements made by an employer to provide a certain amount of money when the worker retires, as a pension; or if the worker dies, as a lump sum; and/or as a widow's, widower's or dependant's pension' (Ward, 1981, p. 3). They can be paid for entirely by the employer, or the employee can also pay a contribution into the scheme's fund; benefits are paid from these contributions and from the revenues generated by the fund's investments. The schemes are intended to supplement the basic state pension. Under the 1975 Social Security Pensions Act all employed people must be either contracted in or out of the state additional (earnings-related) scheme, though in some cases they may belong both to a company scheme and to the state additional scheme.[1] The relationship between the occupational sector and the state sector has always been complex and occasionally fraught, but the focus here is on the management of the former and I shall refer only very occasionally to the state sector.[2]

Two further introductory remarks may be made about what this book does not cover. On the one hand, I have little to say about the adequacy of benefit levels as such. In one sense, of course, this question underlies the whole of the discussion, since the universally agreed objective of pension schemes is to enable their members to enjoy a decent standard of living in their old age. There are major disagreements at every level about how this is to be achieved, ranging from theoretical discussion of the role of finance capital in the UK economy to detailed assessments of the mechanics of pensions administration. It would be nice to be able to report on how member participation affects the level of benefits; even nicer to be able to demonstrate that it materially improves them. But the system is so complex, and the intervening variables so numerous, that only the most impressionistic of judgements is as yet possible. Moreover, the problem of how to decide on the fairness of pensions provision is fiendishly complex. That there are major injustices is obvious, but to bring the divergent interests and claims within a common framework is another matter. Roll together the most calculating of actuaries; the shrewdest of financial analysts; the toughest of negotiators; and the most perceptive of social critics: if the mixture did not instantly combust their combined wisdom would still leave queues of people with more or less legitimate complaints about the way they were being treated or the way their money was being used.

Secondly, I do not deal in depth with the more purely economic aspects of pension funds. Some of the most salient issues are raised – for example, the relationship between the funds' behaviour and economic stability – but theoretical questions on the behaviour of finance capital are not covered. In part this is quite simply because I cannot pretend to be qualified in this field (which puts me, comfortingly or not, in the company of most of the trustees formally responsible for the funds). A more orthodox justification is that the book aims at shedding light on participation as it occurs in the routine management of the schemes. Of course, such routines are shaped by the character of economic management in contemporary capitalist society, as well as by such other factors as the form of the British welfare state. But I do not believe that analyses of power and its distribution are only coherent if they are always directly related to these broader issues. There are different levels of understanding which do not necessarily rise to a particular theoretical peak. Moreover, as I argue later, the very term 'capitalism' is given a fresh complexion by the emergence of pension funds and other institutions. That said, the description and analysis presented here call for other accounts which use wider-angle lenses, and which address themselves directly to the broader political economy of pension funds.

The Management of Age: Trends in Retirement

Demographic projections are notorious for their unreliability, as birth and mortality rates change with unforeseen rapidity. Social habits such as the age at which people marry and have children alter, with women showing a greater attachment to the labour market and a greater determination to establish at least the beginnings of a career before starting a family. Nevertheless, and medical 'breakthroughs' notwithstanding, we should know with a fair degree of certainty how many old people will be alive in the next two decades. The great expansion in their numbers will come as the post-war baby boom generation ages early in the next century, and lives longer than preceding generations. In the OECD countries elderly people (defined as those over 65) averaged 12 per cent of the total population in 1980; this is expected to rise to 13.5 per cent in 2000 and 18 per cent of the total in 2025. In so far as growth in the elderly population is seen as a problem, therefore, we can expect major strains emanating simply from population trends.

The likely significance of these trends for pensions policy depends both on the level or generosity of projected benefits and on the so-called age-dependency ratio: the number of economically active people per pensioner. In the UK this ratio has fallen from 6.6 in 1901 to 2.6 in 1981. It is projected to remain roughly at this level for the next three decades but then to fall further to between 2.0 and 1.4 by the year 2030, as the number of pensioners rises from 10 million to between 14 and 19 million (Haberman, 1985). The combination of more older people and higher benefit levels can result in some intimidating extrapolations. The number of those in receipt of occupational pensions is forecast to rise from its current level of about 4 million to between 6 and 7 million early in the next century, and the average size of the occupational pension from about one-fifth to over one-third of average earnings. The Government Actuary's projections prepared for the Wilson Committee on the functioning of financial institutions showed expenditure on occupational pensions rising from £3.95 billion (1978 prices) in 1975 to £9.4 billion in 2000 (Wilson Committee, 1980, p. 529). On the assumption that schemes will earn a real rate of return of 3 per cent annually, liabilities of all funded schemes will by then total £147 billion (*ibid.* p. 531).[3]

However, amidst this welter of statistics and timescales the 'problem' needs to be set firmly in perspective. In the first place, the elderly population has grown far more rapidly in previous generations than it is growing now, or than it is projected to grow in future decades. Table 1.1 shows the pattern of change throughout this century. Although the proportion of the population aged over 60 will continue to grow, the *rate* of change is far lower than it was between 1920 and 1950. Secondly, the very use of terms such as 'age-dependency ratio' is more than a little tendentious. It encourages the view of older people as passive dependents, a burden on the rest of society. It pushes to one side the fact that the great majority of them have worked for all or most of their lives, paying taxes and pension contributions on the understanding that they would receive a decent standard of living at the end of their working lives. To stigmatise them as dependent implies a fairly cynical view of intergenerational solidarity, and in so far as they are passive this is often a function of the social roles imposed upon them and of the employment policies practised by both public and private sectors.

Moreover, the simple numerical ratio between workers and nonworkers is only a very partial guide to the size and nature of the problem. It is the amount of wealth which is produced and the policies adopted towards its distribution between different classes and age-groups which are crucial. If we leave aside for the moment the issue of unemployment, we can see that the relative numbers involved are irrelevant: the important question is the size of the pie and the way it is divided, rather than the number of people actively involved in making it. If one person and a mass of robots can generate the same level of wealth as the whole of the current working population, then there need be no problem – at least as far as the income levels are concerned. In short, the size of the elderly population is certainly significant, especially in its implications for health policy and especially given that the numbers of very old people (over 75)

Table 1.1: Persons aged 60 or more at census dates

Census year	Total (millions)	As percentage of population	Decennial change %
1901	2.9	7.6	
1911	3.3	7.8	+14
1921	4.3	9.8	+30
1931	5.4	11.7	+26
1941[1]	6.7	13.9	+24
1951[1]	8.0	15.8	+19
1961	8.9	16.9	+11
1971	10.0	18.0	+12
1981	11.1	18.0	+11
1991[2]	11.8	20.7	+6
2001[2]	16.6	20.0	−2

[1] Mid-year estimates
[2] Projections – Government Actuary's Department
Source: *Social Trends 14* (1984) p. 18

are increasing proportionately even more rapidly. But the issues posed by these trends are ones for practical policy decisions and choices – for social *management* – and not merely for fatalistic projection.

Labour market factors cannot be ignored, and especially not the numbers of people without work. But the projections are based on a chronological divide which looks increasingly implausible. There is a crumbling of the conventional dividing line between active and retired people, provoked principally by the economic crisis and the dramatic surge in unemployment. Since wages have more immediate financial implications than pensions, and unemployment statistics a higher political profile than future social cost predictions, the definition of 'normal' retirement age is being abruptly, if covertly, recast. This has caused havoc in traditional classifications and concepts. The idea of a 'normal' working life lasting to 60 or 65 now looks distinctly outmoded. Table 1.2 shows the changes that have occurred since 1971 in the economic activity rates of men and women over 45. Female participation rates show a rather uneven pattern, with a decline only in the over-60 age-group and a marked increase in the 45–54 year olds. By contrast male rates have dropped dramatically, especially for the group nearing formal retirement age, whose participation rate has gone down by 23 points in 12 years. These official statistics, moreover, understate the extent to which people have effectively left the labour force, since older workers who become unemployed are, though formally available for work, in many cases unlikely ever to get a job again. Many have been left in a limbo land: not employed, not retired (in the sense that they do not yet qualify for a

Table 1.2: Civilian labour force economic activity rates 1971–1983 (%)

	Males 45–59	60–64	65+	Females 45–54	55–59	60+
1971	94.8	82.9	19.3	62.0	50.9	12.7
1976	94.9	80.4	14.5	66.5	54.3	10.3
1979	93.8	73.0	10.3	67.0	53.8	7.4
1981	93.0	69.4	10.3	68.1	53.4	8.3
1983	90.2	59.5	8.4	68.3	50.8	8.1

Source: *Social Trends 15* (1985), Table 4.3

state pension) – and often not even formally unemployed, since they are discouraged from registering as such.

One example of change in the social categories involved in the management of age comes from France. In 1981 the incoming (Socialist) administration adopted a policy of encouraging older workers to leave the labour force early explicitly to make room for younger workers on a one-for-one basis. The rationale was to unite society behind the common objective of tackling unemployment, especially youth unemployment – hence the title 'contrats de solidarité'. Together with broader social trends, it has given rise to a new 'generation' of people who have ceased work well before what had been considered 'normal' retirement age. They have been termed the 'demi-vieux', or members of the 'second age', the third age being the able-bodied pensioners beyond 'normal' retirement age, and the fourth wholly dependent old people – leaving the 'first age' to cover all ages up to and even beyond 50, a curiously portmanteau category. In practical terms, these measures have contributed to the covert exclusion of older people from employment and a major but largely unremarked shift in their social circumstances, which Xavier Gaullier (1982) has described as 'la révolution silencieuse'. The categories we use to describe people are undergoing substantial change in the face of pressures whose longer-term effects are hard to predict.

In most European countries the tendency to use early retirement as a means of restructuring the labour force is evident. In broad terms, older workers have historically been used as a crude (and ineffective) regulator of the labour market. Like women, they are encouraged to participate in times of labour shortage, and are fairly quickly extruded when they seem to be in competition for jobs with others whose entitlement to employment is regarded as stronger. Phillipson (1983) has identified three main waves over the last five decades in the UK. Before the Second World War, older people were labelled as relatively feeble, not to be valued as workers at a time when labour was available in such abundance. After the war, labour was in short supply and little money available for social expenditure on pensions, so the older age-group was encouraged to stay at work as long as possible – 'the elderly as producers'. Recently, the re-emergence of mass unemployment has meant a reversion to the exclusionary approach, as both government and employers seek the most convenient way of reducing the official labour force. The government makes subsidies available to speed up early retirement (for instance under the Job Release Scheme), and allows the older unemployed to receive benefits without formally registering as unemployed. Employers seek out those willing to take early retirement and tighten up recruitment policies, so that older workers stand minimal chances of regaining employment once they leave or lose a job.

Just how clearcut these waves are is a matter of judgement, but the pattern may be broadly similar in other countries. In France, for example, Guillemaud (1984) points also to a three-fold pattern over roughly comparable periods. In contemporary times at least it is clear that government, employers and in most cases trade unions see a lowering of the retiring age, *de facto* or officially, as a means of reducing the huge imbalance between the number of those who would like to work and the number of jobs available. Various means are used to this end: financial incentives, direct force or the cultivation of the 'good innings' ethic: the feeling that older people should make way for younger workers. Even in Sweden, with its tradition of strong labour market policies linked with a highly developed awareness of social disadvantage, the experience is similar:

> Although the Swedish partial pension system was originally created not as an instrument of manpower policy but rather as a way of easing the psychological adjustment to retirement and reducing the workload of older workers, ... in practice it has served somewhat different ends. In a difficult economic situation, the 'work sharing' made possible by the introduction of partial retirement was used, by at least half the organisations mentioned, as a means to reduce their labour force without recourse to redundancies. (Casey and Bruche, 1983, p. 44-5)

The objective of most company policies may be crudely summed up as 'reduce and rejuvenate'.

These trends are by no means all negative, socially or economically. The pressure for earlier retirement is easy to understand in the case of physically punishing jobs such as car assembly or coalmining. Many workers are sufficiently disenchanted with their jobs for earlier retirement – official or *de facto* – to be seen as a welcome change. But it is a partial irony that a healthier and longer-living population, employed for the most part in jobs which make fewer demands than in previous times on their physical capabilities, should be led to finish work younger and younger.

Occupational pension schemes have played a substantial part in smoothing this transition. Their original purpose – as we shall explore in more detail in the next chapter – was primarily to ensure a loyal and stable workforce by establishing a benefit which would be lost if the employee changed jobs. The objective remains an important one, as pensions become an increasingly significant component of the 'total remuneration package'. But alongside it is a second objective which appears at first glance to point in the opposite direction: the capacity to reduce the labour force by offering early retirement to older workers who have not yet reached the age of 60 or 65. Occupational schemes give employers greater flexibility in their manpower policy without overtly offending against the social norms which would otherwise constrain their ability to remove older workers from the payroll. This preservation of legitimacy is particularly important in countries where a paternalist tradition forbids the abrupt dislodgement of labour – or at least of indigenous male labour. For example, one of the leading West German employers, Volkswagen, introduced the so-called '59-year regulation', using state support to facilitate early retirement. It proved so effective as an 'adjustment instrument' that it was continued even after the state subsidy was withdrawn, and has been extended downwards to 57 with the prospect of a further lowering of the age-level. It is worth adding as a prelude to our discussion of employee participation that the regulations at Volkswagen, in line with German practice, were jointly agreed between management and the works council.

In the UK the wave of redundancies and manpower reductions in the early 1980s has highlighted the role of pension schemes in easing the transition out of the labour force – a kind of inverted midwifery. Once the transition is accepted, and given the general unavailability of the state pension before the official retiring age, the cushion of an occupational pension is often an important shock-absorber. For those involved in its management, this can be a very significant advantage and a genuine demonstration of a humane personnel policy. In the Glasgow research (see Appendix for details) one pensions manager, sincerely committed to maximising the welfare of his scheme's members, described his satisfaction in being able to relieve some of the fears of employees suddenly confronted with the prospect of early retirement: 'The redundancy exercise has gone far more smoothly than the company could have imagined, because of our early retirement arrangements. The look of complete relief on the faces of individuals has been a joy to behold – "at least we've been looked after".'

Pensions schemes, then, are caught up in the turbulence of social and employment fluctuations, immediate and longer term. They can be criticised for accentuating those fluctuations, or weakening the struggle to maintain employment levels. But they may also be welcomed as stabilisers, creating a greater measure of security for individuals than would otherwise be available.

The Management of Capital: Growth in Pension Fund Assets
The second element which has focussed attention on pension schemes is the spectacular growth in their assets. Many people who have as yet no personal interest in pension levels and little interest in the economic and social problems of ensuring a decent standard of living for the elderly have been struck by the growing concentration of economic wealth.

There is still only a limited understanding of the behaviour of pension funds as owners and investors. In the US as long ago as 1959 Adolf Berle picked up the theme of the shifting balance between owners and managers which he had tackled over twenty years previously, with Gardiner Means. He remarked:

> The holdings of common stock are gradually – or perhaps rather rapidly – beginning to be concentrated in the professional managers of the pension trust funds and the mutual funds ... In terms of law, nothing apparently has changed. The corporation is still the familiar corporation. The stockholder is still the stockholder. His rights are the same as before. His vote is still a vote. The new element is that the stockholders' votes have now been more or less permanently concentrated in a relatively small number of institutions – pension trusts and (to a far lesser extent) insurance companies and mutual funds. (1959, pp. 52-3)

The failure of others in the US to follow Berle's pointers was remarked upon by Drucker:

> The Congress of the United States spent more than two years on the Pension Reform Act of 1974, heard countless witnesses, conducted dozens of studies, and considered a raft of alternative proposals. But there is not one mention in those thousands of printed pages of the social or political implications of the pension funds, and even very little concern for their economic impact on the capital markets or on capital formation. (1976, pp. 9-10)

There was, even so, some specific work on pension funds in the US – see Malca, 1975 and Litvak, 1981 – and Rifkin and Barber brought the issue on to the political scene with the strikingly titled *The North Will Rise Again: Pensions, Politics and Power in the 1980s*.[4] In the UK the level of attention paid to pension funds and their potential power was much lower until quite recently, though in a pamphlet published in 1960 Richard Titmuss referred to 'the explosion in the accumulation of immense funds in the hands of private insurance companies and pension trusts' (1960, p. 13). In a broader context, Anthony Crosland briefly discussed the growth of institutional shareholders in *The Conservative Enemy*, published in 1962. He was interested in the changing relationship between ownership and control and its implications for political theory and practice. But observing that in 1957 pension funds held only 1 per cent of the quoted capital of large companies he held that the prospect of the Berle thesis applying to the UK was rather remote: 'The prospective growth of pension funds ... is not likely to make any substantial difference in the basic control position over these companies which their managements have long held' (1962, p. 77). He therefore dismissed pension funds as irrelevant to his thesis of an almost complete separation of ownership and control, and to the broader question of the relationship between public and private ownership.

By the mid-1970s, however, roaring inflation had increased the size of the funds dramatically. Economic instability and the stock market bubble and crash of 1973/4 sent shivers round the corporate world; pension funds were involved both in pushing up property prices spectacularly and in attempting to prevent the total collapse of stockmarket prices and a whole range of industrial and financial enterprises.[5] One result was the setting up of the Wilson Committee to consider the workings of the financial institutions, whose conclusions are discussed briefly later (p. 15). Yet analysis of the role of pension funds in national economic performance remained (and remains) scanty.[6] Partly, it is fair to say, this is because economists' models seem inadequate to handle the behaviour of such huge corporate entities, acting neither autonomously nor in full concert with each other and with their own set of financial habits. It was not until Richard Minns published *Pension Funds and British Capitalism* (1980) that the outline of substantial empirical work emerged.[7]

The market value of total pension fund assets has rocketed from £4.5 billion in 1963 to £106 billion twenty years later. Table 1.3 shows the increase over the last five years of the period; the assets are at the time of writing growing by about £20 billion annually. Most of these assets (about 58 per cent of the total) are held by private-sector pension schemes, the rest by local-authority (14 per cent) and other public-sector schemes (28 per cent). Table 1.4 illustrates their rise in comparison with other owners.

In 1963 pension funds owned under 7 per cent of UK equities, compared with the 54 per cent which belonged to individual investors and the 10 per cent of insurance companies. By 1975 the funds had

Table 1.3: Total pension fund holdings, 1978–1983 (£ billion)

	1978	1980	1983
British government securities	7.6	11.5	21.8
UK company securities	16.7	25.1	48.1
Overseas company and government securities	1.7	4.4	15.7
UK land and property	4.9	8.2	11.0
Other	3.4	10.7	9.6
Total	34.3	59.9	106.2

Source: *British Business* 15:1 (September 1984)

Table 1.4: Distribution of UK shareholdings by market value (%)

	1963	1975	1981	1983*
Individuals	54.0	37.5	28.2	25.0
Insurance companies	10.0	15.9	20.5	22.0
Banks and investment trusts	12.6	11.2	7.1	6.0
Pension funds	6.4	16.8	26.7	29.0
Other	17.0	18.6	17.5	18.0
Total value of all shareholdings (100%)	£27.7bn	£41.5bn	£99.4bn	£145.0bn

* Estimated
Sources: 1963–81, *Stock Exchange Survey of Share Ownership* (1981); 1983 Phillips and Drew estimates

overtaken the insurance companies, with 16.8 per cent of the total compared with the latter's 15.9 per cent, and had closed the gap very considerably on individual investors (37.5 per cent). Only eight years further on and they had established themselves as clear leaders, with an estimated 29 per cent, as individual shareholdings tumbled to 25 per cent of the total. Clearly such trends can be used to generate absurd projections of the funds gobbling up the whole of British industry by the turn of the century. But even if their appetite is abruptly sated, their position as major repositories of shareholder capital is unmistakable.

The funds' holdings in other sectors are also substantial, although they do not dominate to quite the same extent. In the gilt-edged market insurance companies are the principal holders of medium- and long-dated stocks with 34 per cent of the total in 1982, but pension funds also held one-quarter of the total. Property is the other major area of investment. Between 1971 and 1978, for example, the City's financial institutions increased their farmland holdings from 50 000 to 530 000 acres, and the increasing capital dependence of British agriculture reflects the growing pressure of pension funds and their sister-institutions, their udders bursting with the daily influx of new money. Although the funds have reduced their holdings in property from the peak of 1981 (when over 17 per cent of the assets of private sector funds were in property), they are by any standards massive owners of both buildings and land (Norton-Taylor, 1982).

It is not only the sheer size of the funds which has aroused comment. One of the most striking aspects of investment patterns over the last five years has been the flow of capital overseas since exchange controls were lifted by the incoming Conservative administration in 1979. Initially it was projected that there would be a sharp movement of capital to other countries in the first year or two, but that this would soon level off as funds reached a 'natural' ceiling in the amount they were willing to invest abroad. Currency risks would deter investment managers from going much over 10 per cent in the proportion they placed overseas. Instead the flow was substantial and continuous up to the end of 1983.

Although it appeared to have tapered off and even been reversed by early 1984, by the third quarter the flow had resumed, so that total net investment in overseas company securities was £475 million in the second half of the year (*British Business, 16:13*, April 1985). A steady stream had been replaced by turbulent flux. The impact of these massive movements of capital is uncertain. One view is that they are highly damaging to UK economic performance, increasing uncertainty, raising interest rates unnecessarily and impeding long-term investment. A contrary view is that the export of capital merely reflects market forces and is the consequence rather than a cause of poor performance and low profitability. The economists show little sign of reaching a consensus, but concern is spreading over the longer-term effects of such instability. The point here is that the debate is likely to become more vocal and to impinge forcefully on those responsible for managing the funds.[8]

The growth of funds coincided with the accentuation of Britain's economic problems. In the late 1960s it was held in some quarters that poor industrial relations and the bloody-mindedness of British workers were primarily responsible for the country's poor post-war economic performance. Following the Donovan Report on trade union and employer associations in 1968, the Labour government and its Conservative successor focussed their attention on this aspect, though without conspicuous success. But the individual or collective characteristics of labour could not be plausibly made to bear sole responsibility for economic decline. Increasingly throughout the 1970s, lack of investment was identified as a major factor in declining British competitiveness, as British factories and workers struggled to make do with outdated plant and equipment. Self-doubt and low morale are easy prey for simplistic, single-factor explanations, and lack of capital investment is only one of a number of interacting elements. But the queries prompted by concern over economic performance led logically to public interest in the sources of capital potentially available for the restructuring of British industry, and pension funds came in for their share of the limelight.

The Wilson Committee was set up in 1977 to review the workings of financial institutions. It discussed the idea that there was in Britain a general shortage of finance for investment. The simplistic argument which holds that the root cause of Britain's economic ills is a lack of capital investment without referring to the terms on which it is made available or to the factors which shape the demand for it was substantially demolished. The Committee's conclusions have often been interpreted subsequently as giving 'a clean bill of health' to the financial institutions. Yet the Committee made a number of critical comments. It noted that 'areas of concern certainly exist as to whether the greater presence of the institutions has been a cause of increased market volatility, and as to whether the investment policies of the institutions unduly discriminate against smaller or high risk companies' (1980, p. 193). There was particular concern about the adequacy of finance 'where there is a lengthy period before positive returns can be expected' - one of a number of comments on the short-run focus of the present system. The Committee suggested (p. 259) that 'the rapid development of life assurance and pension funds over the last 20 years has thrust considerable responsibilities upon them', in the light of which they might be interpreting their fiduciary obligations too narrowly, a point of key importance when we come to consider the role of trustees and the constraints on them (Chapter 6). Finally the Committee suggested that a new regulatory framework was needed for occupational pension schemes. Disagreeing with this suggestion three years later, the then Governor of the Bank of England nevertheless observed that 'among major financial institutions, self-administered pension funds are least subject to official prudential supervision' (Richardson, 1983, p. 508). Investment behaviour, long-term orientation, new responsibilities and an adequate system of regulation: this is a fairly substantial agenda for continued diagnosis and prescription.

I shall return to the ramifying debate on the control of capital in Chapter 5. For the moment it is enough to have sketched out the mammoth contours of the funds, before we turn to look in more detail at who or what determines the path their footprints take as they tramp across the quaking bog of the British economy. Apart from the general interest in the impact of their behaviour on investment patterns and economic performance, there are two sets of parties with particular interests. First, individual members and their representatives are concerned with the impact of their own fund's performance on their benefit levels and options, as well as with the accountability of the scheme's management to themselves as putative owners. Secondly, company managements have been alerted to the cost implications of pension obligations and to the problems of managing assets which may well outstrip those of the company itself. These are the principal participants in the process of decision-making at company level.

Democratic Management: The Background of Participation

Chimera, panacea, busted flush: employee participation is a phenomenon which constantly recurs in different guises, and is given different values. Broadly defined it refers to the involvement of working people in decisions which affect their working lives. One range of terms, widely used to capture this diversity, runs from consultation at one end to workers' control at the other on a sliding scale of power distribution between labour and capital (for example Coates and Topham, 1974). The first of these, consultation, implies little more than that workers are informed of managerial decisions before they are implemented. They have the right to make their views known, but no power to insist that these are effectively taken into account. Schemes which operate on this basis can be critically assessed as pseudo-participation (Pateman, 1970), offering only an illusory involvement in decision-making. But not all consultation is fraudulent: even where management explicitly retains the unilateral right to decide, it may pay serious attention to the views of the workforce, as a means of pre-empting disruptive discontent if nothing else. The spectrum proceeds along a line of mounting employee influence to the point where workers take all decisions themselves, with capital having no rights *per se*. In Coates and Topham's terminology this is workers' self-management; beyond this lies workers' control, where ownership as well as control is vested in labour.

Other classifications focus on different aspects (Schuller, 1985, Chapter 1). They may distinguish direct participation from that which takes place through some form of representative structure, or refer to types of decision involved. Wall and Lischeron (1977), for example, distinguish between distant, medium and immediate decisions: the former relate to strategic issues such as capital investment programmes, the latter to issues which have immediate implications for employees' working conditions. The legal status of participative arrangements is another dimension: the IDE group refer to *de jure* and *de facto* forms of participation, according to whether they have an explicit constitutional basis or are more a matter of custom and practice (1981). Representation may be exercised through recognised trade union channels, or in parallel to them. In the latter case, participation may be seen as a threat to trade union organisation, even a deliberate attempt to undermine it: the spread of Japanese-inspired quality circles is one of a range of employer initiatives to reduce union bargaining power in its traditional forms. But it may be seen as a legitimate complement to collective bargaining, allowing a plurality of exchange and interaction between workers and management. And collective bargaining can itself be regarded as a major form of participation, especially where it goes beyond the traditional areas of pay and conditions and brings other issues under a degree of joint regulation (see Chapter 3).

All of these categories may be applied fruitfully to the analysis of pension scheme participation. The length of the list reflects the diversity of daily routines at workplaces up and down the country. The diversity is compounded by mergers and takeovers leading to organisational structures of labyrinthine complexity. Individual workplaces are not necessarily any bigger than they used to be but they are more likely to form part of an organisation which spreads across industries, regions and even countries. Sometimes there is a degree of intrinsic business logic to the proliferation, for example where it brings about a vertical integration of the several stages of the production process. But in other cases – especially in the UK – the sole co-ordinating factor is finance. The organisation's diverse activities do not belong to each other in any sense other than that they appeal, perhaps only temporarily, to those who control its overall balance sheet. As a result, bargaining and participation structures in large organisations are often themselves very complex, reflecting multiple horizontal and vertical divisions. It is often extremely difficult to identify the seat of decision-making, especially on strategic issues. The rash of mergers within the financial sector and the tightening links between banks and large corporations give an added twist to this complex pattern (see Chapter 5).

In the light of this, what are the prospects for extending effective participation? One of the most frequently quoted observations on the experience of participation is that of Blumberg: 'There is scarcely a study in the entire literature which fails to demonstrate that satisfaction at work is enhanced or that other generally acknowledged beneficial consequences accrue from a genuine increase in workers' decision-making' (1968, p. 123). The combination of moral appeal and economic functionalism (participation is good in itself and good for business) might seem to imply that there is a rational inevitability to workers achieving a greater measure of influence at work. A long- or short-term historical glance is enough to reveal this as a simplistic illusion. Enthusiasm and action over participation is not quite a matter of ephemeral fashion with no solid residue, but there is certainly no irreversible progression.

Events over the last decade illustrate this sharply. In 1974 a Labour government came to power. Almost its first act was to pass the Trade Union and Labour Relations Act, which strengthened the bargaining rights of the trade unions and the opportunities for union representatives to organise and educate themselves. In the following year the Health and Safety at Work Act gave recognised union representatives the right to require that a joint committee should be set up to deal with health and safety issues. The 1975 Employment Protection Act further consolidated the basis on which union representatives could enter into effective negotiations on a widening range of issues. On the bargaining side, therefore, the basis for a significant extension of participation seemed to be laid, though there were already doubts whether trade unions were showing themselves to be sufficiently adaptable and far-sighted to give this basis effective legitimacy.

Another substantial step, this time at the level of strategic decision-making, seemed imminent when the Bullock Committee on industrial democracy was set up in 1975. Its remit was specifically to consider how, not whether, the introduction of worker directors on to company boards might be accomplished. Although the report bore the all-embracing title of 'Industrial Democracy', it was concerned almost exclusively with representation at board level. The Report's principal recommendation was for worker directors to be elected to the boards of major companies (those with over 2000 employees), equal in number to shareholder representatives. A smaller, odd, number of directors were also to be appointed from outside the company, to avoid the possibility of deadlock between managerial and worker directors. This was the famous $2x + y$ formula.

So by 1977, when the Bullock Report appeared, there seemed to be both a consolidation and an extension of employee influence of significant dimensions. In addition, the government had published a White Paper recommending mandatory representation on the boards of pension funds, with equal numbers from employees and the company, the former to be drawn through recognised union channels. We shall come back to this in more detail later. For the moment, it is enough to show that it fitted into an apparent pattern of greater rights of representation. Yet the setting up of the Bullock Committee can hardly be portrayed as part of a planned strategy to shift the balance of power fundamentally in favour of labour. It was, as Elliott (1978) has recounted, as much an accident of parliamentary procedure as anything else. The reception of its report would already have been enough to arouse doubts about the strength of support for it and about the steady progress towards greater democracy at work. Not surprisingly there was vociferous opposition from business spokesmen (concerted, moreover, since the Report's main thrust was known well beforehand). But there was little sustained and convincing support for the proposals from labour. Energetically though the signatories of the majority report (the business representatives had dissented and produced a minority report) deployed their arguments up and down the country, the lack of widespread enthusiasm deprived their recommendations of political impetus. At a time when the government was running into major economic storms and when relations with the unions were under severe strain as the result of prolonged income restraint, no senior politician was eager to fight for the implementation of the recommendations and there was no sustained pressure from the unions to do so.[9]

Simplifying greatly, there were two main reasons for this. First, although Jack Jones, General Secretary of the powerful Transport and General Workers Union, had succeeded in securing the TUC's formal commitment to the notion of worker directors, and in shaping the remit of the Committee so that it considered how rather than whether they should be introduced, there was a lack of convinced grassroots support for the proposals. It is not always true that a collective mind can only be changed gradually, but on this occasion it proved to be the case. Employees generally, and a good number of union officials and leaders, did not show themselves ready to support a major initiative which departed from the conventional model of collective bargaining. The second reason is closely related. Had the contemporary economic crisis been less pronounced the report could maybe have been more widely sold; but wage claims took absolute priority at the time: few union representatives relished the prospect of suggesting to their members, after three years of wage restraint, that they should concentrate on the longer-term strengthening of their influence rather than immediate pay rises.

From 1978 onwards, labour was increasingly on the defensive, both politically and on the shop floor. Not only were the proposals for worker directors first watered down as a consequence of the political pact with the Liberals and then summarily discarded by the Conservative government elected in 1979; the supposed equalisation of bargaining power was quickly eroded, by direct legislation but even more so by economic trends.

Most obviously the huge upsurge in unemployment, from 1.3 million in 1979 to over 3 million (even on official statistics) in 1985, dramatically affected the prospects for participation and attitudes to it. The living standards of those in work have continued to improve, opening up an ever-widening gap between them and those without jobs. Employee participation has little meaning for the unemployed. Within the ranks of the employed, a polarisation has begun to emerge between core groups of employees with relative security and a growing periphery of workers employed on a contract or part-time basis, often poorly organised and with little job security. For the former, a measure of participation may be part of their core status, whilst the latter have little opportunity to influence decisions or even to take part in orthodox union affairs. In general, people are more concerned with keeping their jobs than pressing for greater participation.

Major divisions have opened up within the industrial arm of the labour movement, as the 1984 miners' strike showed; this has substantially reduced the momentum behind any concerted move towards new or extended forms of employee influence. The acceptance by some unions of no-strike agreements is just one example of the way the balance has shifted. The forward march of labour, in collective bargaining and in other forms of participation, seemed by then to have been joltingly halted. 'Participation' itself has been the subject of reinterpretation. Profit-sharing schemes are just one example of the way the Conservative government and many managements have sought to redefine the issue as one of individual employee involvement, removing the links between the employee and any form of collective organisation.

Will the wheel turn again? On one interpretation, there is historically a cyclical pattern to interest in worker participation (see, for example, Ramsay, 1977). It rises at times such as post-war crises, when there is economic and moral pressure to offer war heroes something attractive enough to smooth the path to recovery, or at times of labour shortage. But it dies away or is actively cut short when employers, including the state, no longer regard it as functional. There is force behind this analysis, especially in the way it offers both a historical context and a dynamism of approach. But the image of a cycle is too fixed and symmetrical, implying the tidy repetition of a fixed sequence. Instead, as I have already suggested elsewhere (Schuller, 1985, Chapter 3), the rhythm of tidal activity may be more apt. For whilst it too is repetitive, tidal activity is in itself often varied and turbulent; moreover, it changes the contours of the landscape and sea bottom, sometimes quite drastically. In short, a survey of participation over the last decade would certainly have to point to a rise and fall of governmental support for union-based representation in strategic company decision-making. On the other hand, the movement has not all been in one dimension. There are, at the very least, eddies and counterflows within the ebb tide. To take just a few examples, consultative committees have survived and grown, for all the ambiguity over their actual impact; health and safety committees are firmly established, even if the scope and impact of activities are cramped by the recession; some trade unions are reorganising themselves and taking longer-term perspectives; more vaguely, the European Community's directives on participation and on information disclosure within large enterprises struggle onwards. There is also the topic of this book: the emergence of pensions decision-making as an area where collective bargaining has been extended and employee representation at the strategic level of decision-making introduced.

Notes

1. The occupational system is sometimes referred to as the 'private' sector of pensions, though it includes the occupational schemes of nationalised industries and other public employees as well as those of privately owned industry and commerce.
2. The whole question of the partnership between the occupational and the state sectors has been raised by the publication in 1985 of a Government Green Paper on the reform of social security (DHSS, 1985). One of the main proposals is that SERPS, the state earnings-related pension scheme, should over a number of years be replaced by 'personal pensions' for those who are not in an occupational pension scheme. The proposal is surrounded by uncertainties and divergent projections about the economic and organisational implications of the proposal. At the time of writing its future is not settled. All that can be said here is that the abolition of SERPS would add very substantially to the complexity and cost of managing occupational schemes, as people move between personal and occupational schemes and collective coverage is fragmented.
3. Alongside this, as the state earnings-related pension scheme (SERPS) comes gradually into full operation, contributions to pay for it and the basic scheme are officially estimated to rise from 12.5 per cent of gross earnings to nearly 20 per cent by 2025. This type of projection lies behind the government's proposal to abolish SERPS (see note 2), but there is no consensus on how big a share of the economy SERPS would take. For other countries, the implications of equivalent projections on pensions expenditure are spectacular: West Germany, for instance, is faced with the possibility of an increase in the payroll tax to almost one-third of the gross wage over the next 50 years simply to maintain current benefits – and that on optimistic assumptions of overall growth rates (*Economist*, 19 May 1984).
4. The central argument of the book was that the pension funds of workers in the smokestack industries in the north-east of the United States were being used, largely unaccountably, to generate economic growth in the non-unionised southern states, thereby contributing to the destruction of the jobs of those to whom the fund belonged. The book raises many of the issues discussed below in Chapters 5 and 6.
5. See Plender (1982, Chapters 5 and 6) and Reid (1982). The funds' role in rescuing the national economy from the disasters threatened by the secondary bank crisis of the mid-1970s should be remembered when current arguments are considered about whether or not they have obligations which go beyond the immediately defined interests of their own members (see Chapters 5 and 6).
6. For example, the first edition (1976) of Leslie Hannah's book *The Rise of the Corporate Economy*, widely recognised as admirably thorough, contains chapters on 'Capitalist Ownership and The Stock Market' and 'The Modern Corporate Economy' but makes no mention at all of pension funds.
7. For a review of some relevant research on economic aspects of the issue, see Artus and Minto (1984).
8. As in other aspects, the funds are part of a wider pattern involving other financial institutions. The pattern is further complicated – and the question of overseas investment along with it – by the fact that the largest companies, in which pension fund money is heavily concentrated, organise much of their production and place much of their money overseas. The largest 50 UK companies base nearly 40 per cent of their production in foreign countries, and overseas acquisitions by UK companies increased ten-fold between 1977 and 1981.
9. At the time of Bullock, direct experience of worker directors in the UK was limited largely to that of the British Steel Corporation, plus a few isolated instances in the private sector (Brannen, Batstone, Fatchett and White, 1976). One concrete result was the initiation of an experimental period with worker directors in the Post Office; including the preliminary negotiations needed to get the scheme under way the experiment covered nearly four years but the worker directors actually sat for just two years. The process was monitored by a team from Warwick University. Their conclusions did nothing to confirm the fears expressed of disastrous consequences

and immobilised decision-making but suggested also that the impact on strategic decisions was limited in the extreme (Batstone, Ferner and Terry, 1983).

2 From Gratuity to Deferred Pay

There was no proper pension scheme until after the Second World War. Before then it was up to the Vesteys to decide whether an employee would receive anything when he became too old to work. A former manager explains how the system worked: 'I remember a manager in the twenties, who was getting about £700 a year, going to the Vesteys about his retirement. He was offered a pound or two a week. They'd want to know all about your family history. Was your wife dead or alive? Any children? Daughter? Is she married? No? Then she can keep you. No, I'm not depending on my daughter and I can't manage on a pound a week. You'd have to make your case and try and get a bit more. Perhaps if the offer was a pound you might get thirty shillings.' (Knightley, 1981, pp. 23-4)

Public attitudes towards pension schemes have changed over the past few years. What was once regarded as an incentive to long and loyal service is increasingly regarded as a right for which employees have contributed. Indeed, many people regard pensions as deferred pay. (DHSS, 1984, p. 3)

This chapter begins by tracing out the growth of occupational pensions and the evolution of attitudes towards them. From being a benefit restricted to a small minority they have become a widespread feature of conditions of employment. Moreover, the status of the benefit has undergone a complete transformation. From being in most sectors an *ex gratia* payment, with the employer often deciding not only how much was to be paid but even whether any such payment would be made at all, it has become an entitlement, as the DHSS memorandum quoted above indicates. As we shall explore in this and subsequent chapters, the question of who should control this entitlement is still far from settled; but that it is a right is very widely accepted.

As with many other areas of social policy, the history of pensions (state and occupational) is characterised by a marked degree of arbitrariness and haphazard growth.[1] It has been shaped by a mixture of successive governments' sensitivities (or lack of them) to employment and unemployment levels, to expenditure implications and to the views of pressure groups or advisers; often confused or ill-thought-out notions of fairness and efficiency; and a variety of sometimes contradictory employer strategies and union responses in different industries. Lack of information, the difficulty of grappling with an essentially long-term issue and perhaps also an innate fear of confronting the implications of human ageing, have combined to make the process of policy formation unusually incoherent.[2]

One example is the fixing of the retirement age. A fixed age of 65 was first introduced for the Civil Service in 1859. The goal was to remove those who were thought to be too old to give effective service, but the choice of 65 as the age was based on wholly impressionistic evidence. When a state means-tested non-contributory pension was introduced in 1908 it was paid at 70, contrary to such evidence as existed on the chronology of physical decline. It happened because the Treasury refused to pay the extra cost of pensions at 65 – estimated at £9 million annually rather than £7 million. In 1925 the age was reduced by a Conservative government introducing a contributory scheme, and has in effect remained at 65 ever since for men. In 1940 the age for women was reduced to 60, largely due to the pressure of the National Spinsters Association, despite the fact that women live significantly longer than men. There is now pressure to reduce the male age to 60 (partly to reduce unemployment statistics) or to bring the male age down and the female age up to 62 or 63 simultaneously, to achieve one type of equality at an acceptable level of expense. Flexibility of retirement age is accepted as a good idea but hard to implement. As Pat Thane concluded, commenting on the 'muddled history' of retirement:

> Our present retirement ages thus reflect conditions in the latter part of the nineteenth and early twentieth centuries. Even at that time they probably drew into a new and broader definition of old age many who were by no means decrepit. Since the physical efficiency of old people has certainly improved over this century, it is doubtful whether this definition remains appropriate. People now defined as old may feel 'useless' and marginal to society. This feeling is made more acute by continuing physical vigour. It is a historically new experience, for which some solution is needed. (1978, p. 238)[3]

In other countries too the age at which pensions were to be paid is reported to have been arrived at through a crude parody of actuarial calculation. Introducing a national programme of social security for Germany in the 1880s, in which pensions were included:

> Bismarck asked his advisers to recommend an age for retirement where most people knew someone in their family or community who had

lived to that age but that at the same time there were relatively few of that age so that the cost of the scheme was kept down. Bismarck was more interested in stemming the tide of European revolution than in any soft or sentimental concern for the subjects of the Prussian Empire. (Culverhouse, 1982, p. 20)

The anecdote illustrates the arbitrary way in which what was to become almost universally the 'normal' retirement age was established. But it also illuminates the maintenance of tranquillity as one of the chief motivating factors behind the introduction of pensions – in this case, at state rather than enterprise level.

Occupational pension schemes predate Bismarck. They have evolved 'in an unco-ordinated, and largely unregulated, way' (Richardson, 1983, p. 504). The very earliest ones were in the public sector and constitute an interesting example of an intergenerational contract:

Some government departments had charity funds for the aged and indigent, while annuities and sinecures could be obtained through special influence. But usually it was up to the office-holder to strike a bargain with his would-be successor. The principle that pensions should be a collective responsibility has been traced back to the superannuation fund established by customs officers in the reign of Anne. But it was not generally accepted by the Civil Service until 1810. (Thomas, 1976, p. 242)

The first systematic scheme was introduced in 1834, and occupational pensions remained the prerogative of civil servants until the early part of the next century.[4] Even then, the schemes proliferated largely amongst public-sector employees: teachers in 1918, police in 1921 and firemen in 1925. Local authority employees already had their own schemes in the nineteenth century – with transferability between them, what is more – but they were established on a firmer legal basis in 1937 (and again in 1953). Coverage in the private sector was far more limited at this time, with only 13 per cent of all workers being members of occupational schemes in 1936. The major expansion in the number of scheme members took place over the next twenty years, from 2.5 million in 1936 to 8.3 million in 1956. It was consolidated by the 1959 National Insurance Act which gave companies with sufficiently good pension schemes the right to 'contract out', that is to provide their own pension supplementary to the basic state pension, instead of participating in the additional state scheme, and by the late 1960s over half of all employees were included in some form of occupational pension scheme.

Coverage, however, is very far from complete (see Table 2.1). Figures from the 1983 Government Actuary's survey are not yet available, but it is known that the number of scheme members has actually begun to decline, with a drop of almost a million, to about 11 million, between 1979 and 1983. This largely reflects the fall in overall employment. Equally significantly, the division between those who are included and those who are not has followed the well-worn patterns of advantage and disadvantage. In 1975, for example, coverage ranged from 22 per cent for agricultural workers to 82 per cent for certain groups of non-manual employees. Part-timers and temporary employees are very often excluded, which means in turn that fewer women are covered. Although the proportion of full-time women employees in schemes rose from 53 per cent in 1979 to virtual equivalence with the male level of just over 60 per cent in 1983, the fact that over two in five women employees work part time means that their overall coverage is far lower (62 per cent of the schemes surveyed in a 1984 Equal Opportunities Commission report excluded part-timers, McGoldrick, 1984). The 1979 Government Actuary's Department survey showed 87 per cent coverage for men in the public sector and 60 per cent for women; in the private sector the gap was even more pronounced, with 52 per cent of men covered compared with only 23 per cent of women. Though extensive, therefore, simple coverage is very far from complete (leaving aside variations in the treatment of members themselves in different schemes).

Table 2.1: Numbers of employees in pension schemes (millions)

Year	Private sector	Public sector	Total
1936	1.6	1.0	2.6
1953	3.1	3.1	6.2
1956	4.3	3.7	8.0
1963	7.2	3.9	11.1
1967	8.1	4.1	12.2
1971	6.8	4.3	11.1
1975	6.0	5.4	11.4
1979	6.2	5.6	11.8

Source: Green, 1982

The most evident reason for the expansion of the schemes was not demand from employees or their representatives, but the carrot of fiscal incentive. Tax relief for pensions contributions constituted a powerful motor behind their growth, especially following the Second World War as higher proportions of employees began to pay income tax. On top of the relief for contributions, schemes obtain relief also for lump-sum payments. The effect of this incentive has grown steadily with the complexity of the overall tax system. In 1965 the overall subsidy was £120 million; by 1983 this had grown to something between £1.5 billion and £5 billion annually (the huge variation in the estimates is an indication of the inadequacy of available information).[5]

The other main thrust behind the schemes' expansion was their usefulness as a means of inducing loyalty, or at least compliance, amongst employees. This was closely associated with the bureaucratisation of employment through the growth of large organisations with thousands of employees. In the private sector it was the big employers that developed pension schemes around the turn of the century: alongside the railways (the only business in the nineteenth century to employ over 30 000 people) were industrial giants such as Colman and Lever Brothers. The objective was to strengthen the commitment of employees to the company over their lifetime and as long as they were useful. (In this context it is understandable that pensions were often tied to a mandatory retirement age; the decline in the marginal productivity of older workers made it convenient for companies to be able to compel people to retire (Hannah, 1986, pp. 134–137).[6]

The historical development of company welfare schemes as an instrument of control (equivalent to Bismarck's goal at state level) has been thoroughly documented.[7] Richard Titmuss referred to them as 'the undivided loyalty tranquilliser of the corporation' (1960). There is a danger of excessive functionalism here. In one sense, any offer by an employer can be construed as an attempt to exercise greater control (including the introduction of participation itself if this is seen as an instrument of legitimating the status quo). When the labour market is tight his aim is to retain labour; when it is slack, his aim is to exercise discipline over those who are fortunate enough to be in work. We need, therefore, to observe how the frontiers of control have shifted, and to look at what is being controlled and by whom.

There is a parallel here with the current debate over 'deskilling' and the labour process. Braverman (1974) argued that employers introduce new technologies and systems of work organisation with the direct aim of depriving workers of their occupational skills and hence of their ability to exercise control over their own jobs. This has certainly been one motive in many instances. But to suggest that it is the dominant one – and that it has been universally effective – runs the risk of crediting employers with both omnipotence and omniscience in their desire to control their workforces (Salaman, 1982). Similarly one can exaggerate the extent to which the same motive of control inspired the growth of occupational welfare in general and pension schemes in particular. Employers, public and private, are not always far-sighted schemers and their objectives may be ambiguous and contradictory. Moreover, even if part of the original motivation behind the schemes can be shown to be a desire to maintain a loyal and stable workforce, subsequent developments have meant that their current function and effect must be judged in rather different terms. At the level of social attitudes the emergence of the deferred pay concept means that pensions are no longer regarded as an act of employer benevolence, and the growth of bargaining and member participation has provided potential opportunities for employees to extend their influence into a new area of company policy. The extent of that potential and the degree to which it has been realised are issues that will be looked at in subsequent chapters.

In short, it would be simplistic to argue that employers have always been clear and cynical in their introduction of pension schemes, and that the schemes have continued to serve only their interests. Bearing these reservations in mind, we can identify certain explicit intentions on their part, and point to features of the system which continue to constrain the freedom of employees in ways that go beyond the imperfections to be expected in any complex welfare system.

In the first place, unilateral control of pension entitlements constituted a powerful and potentially punitive instrument, especially at times of industrial unrest. In the nineteenth century the Admiralty's dockyard officers used the award of pensions (and, at the other end of the life-cycle, of apprenticeships) directly to increase its control over the workforce (Pahl, 1984, p. 158). In the private sector, Pilkington's was early in the field with a scheme for manual as well as staff employees. In 1937 one of their directors commented on the use that had been made of this ten years previously: 'There was a supplementary fund controlled and contributed to by the company. This was useful in the General Strike. Benefits were automatically forfeited but men were reinstated with one shilling per week less pension right.'[8] Direct penalisation of this kind is now very rare.[9] But there are other features which were overtly recognised as useful instruments of control and which persist today. The most prominent is the restriction on an employee's freedom to change jobs. For those in more privileged positions and with generous pension provision, this is commonly referred to as the 'golden handcuffs' syndrome; for others, the metal is of a baser kind. Addressing the Association of Superannuation Funds in 1953, the MP H. Watkinson was quite blunt about the rationale: 'I know well enough that the reason why firms introduce pension schemes is to stop just that sort of thing [job-changing]... We have certainly a good deal of evidence that mobility of labour is restricted where there is a fairly tight pension scheme...' A few years later, still in a period of great labour shortage, a Wiggins Teape executive opined: '... that transferability was to be deprecated... believing in pensions as a means of keeping employees with the company'.

Total non-transferability occurs when employees lose all their entitlements if they leave. Often the handcuffs are not locked quite so tightly in that a degree of transferability is allowed. But 'nonpreservation' means that the chink of the chains may still be oppressively loud. Where pension rights are not preserved, early leavers (those who leave company service before retirement age) are penalised by receiving smaller benefits in return for a given number of years' membership than they would have had if they had stayed. To take just one example from the 1981 Occupational Pensions Board report: under normal assumptions of earnings growth, the disloyalty of a person who had just one job change at the age of 45 would cause him or her to achieve only 60 per cent of the pension of an identical person who had stayed in the same job throughout. Before the 1973 Social Security Act there were no statutory rights for preservation, but even now the degree of preservation is far from complete. (The current proposal is for inflation-'proofing' by the rate of inflation or 5 per cent per annum, whichever is the lesser.)

Ironically, the objective of reducing labour mobility by penalising employees for being disloyal enough to change jobs has become something of a millstone around the pension industry's neck. The inequitable treatment of early leavers has attracted criticism of the occupational pensions system from all quarters. A Conservative government pledged to non-intervention in the affairs of industry has promised legislation on this front. Whatever its original usefulness as a means of encouraging employees to think of themselves as company servants for a lifetime, that has now been balanced or even outweighed as scheme membership expanded to include the bulk of the total workforce (and therefore reduce the relative 'privilege' involved) and resentment at the evident inequity and inefficiency has mounted. The irony is compounded by changes in the labour market background: employers probably now complain more about the problems of shifting existing members of their workforce than about the difficulty of retaining them.

Naturally, part of the effect of the schemes still depends on the fact that they are to a degree exclusive. There is in most cases a requirement that employees should serve a minimum period before they are eligible to join the scheme. This period is markedly shorter for white-collar workers, for whom it is normally under six months if it exists at all, than for unskilled workers where it may be up to five years. Rose (1983) argues that since labour turnover is highest amongst the latter category this tells against the view that pension schemes are designed to ensure loyalty. But the point is rather that it is more advantageous to introduce white-collar employees as quickly as possible into the scheme since turnover costs more in their case. The earlier they are in the scheme, the more effective the inducement to loyalty. (They are also generally more sensitive to pension provision.) The difference in minimum service requirements in any case underlines the tendency of occupational schemes to accentuate inequalities between manual workers and salaried staff.

The tendency to inequality is also inherent in another component of control built in to the system: the growing use of final salary as a basis for calculating pensions. This has been one of the most prominent trends of the past decade, as 90 per cent of private-sector schemes are now on a final salary basis, compared with under 25 per cent a quarter of a century ago. (Almost all public-sector schemes are on a final salary basis.) A final salary scheme is one where pensions are calculated as a fraction of the salary earned in the final year (or few years) of service, multiplied by the number of years of service. This clearly favours the higher earners whose pay continues to rise as they get older. It implies in principle that workers who stay with the employer until they retire have their pension rights protected against inflation until that time (though not once they have retired). Where there is a significant level of inflation there is heavy cross-subsidisation of older and longer-serving workers by younger and short-service ones. Where there is low inflation or deferred benefits are index linked, the leavers still lose out to the stayers if incomes rise over their working lives, since the final income is the peak of the lifetime earnings profile. Green (1982) observes that these features admirably serve the function of control, whether or not they were consciously designed for this purpose. Once again there is a danger of functionalism in such an interpretation, as any incentive can in theory be regarded in the same way. But pension schemes are certainly part of an elaborate system with its own defined, if changeable, rules. And as Green concludes, with the evolution of these schemes pension contributions increasingly cease to have the character of saving and take on more the character of a tax or an expense, while pension benefits appear increasingly as deferred pay (1982, p. 273).

No Tax Without Representation

It has taken some time for the current view of pensions as deferred pay to establish itself. In the light of this it is perhaps surprising to find that the principle and practice of employee participation in the management of pensions have a long lineage. Many of the issues are recognised in the remarks of H.W. Manly which are worth quoting at length. Writing in the *Journal of the Institute of Actuaries* in 1901, he concluded that there is an inherent logic to the claim for participation through representation:

> The general principle [of pension funds] is undoubtedly good, and morally sound in the abstract, but it takes no account of the weakness of human nature. The principle that everyone should make a provision for his old age is one that we shall all approve. To encourage this principle, the employer says to his employees: 'If you will all consent to contribute a percentage of your salaries to create a fund for providing pensions in your old age, I will subscribe an equal amount each year'... In this way he feels that he has acted the part of a

philanthropist in encouraging thrift; he thinks that his staff will be more contented and settled, and are not likely to leave him when they have a stake in the fund; and he has allayed an uneasy conscience which half recognised an unpleasant responsibility to help, in his old age, a man who has given him lifelong service. The employee's view of the arrangement is very different. To him the contribution is a hardship and an obnoxious tax; and, although he gave his consent to subscribe, it was an agreement made under moral compulsion. What benefit will it be to him? He will never live to 65! and if he does, he is not going to stick in that firm all his life. He does not see why he should be taxed for the benefit of the old members of the staff, who will be retiring soon. The governors might at least raise their salaries to enable them to pay the tax. And if the employer does take a generous view of the case and raise their salaries, the contribution to the fund does not cease to be a tax. It is always a tax, and is always a very good excuse for asking for increase of salary.

Now, where there is taxation, there should always be representation. (1901, pp. 215-16).

Manly goes on to observe the limitations on this apparent democratic imperative: '...staff are generally invited to elect representatives as managers of the Fund, the employers nominating the trustees and reserving to themselves certain powers'. But the principle of representation, and the basis for it, are quite clearly if grudgingly set out. And the logic of these remarks applies to all pension schemes: non-contributory schemes should be treated as being of the same order as contributory ones (though Manly himself did not accept this). For employees in a non-contributory scheme do not pay directly into the fund; but they naturally see the additional contributions made by the employer on their behalf (compared to a contributory scheme) as being more or less equivalent to the sum he would have been obliged to pay them had the scheme been contributory.[10] Of course, logic does not always prevail and there is no doubt that contributory and non-contributory schemes generate different attitudes to the appropriate balance of control over the scheme and the fund. Employer control has always been strongest – and most strongly legitimated – in non-contributory schemes. But the basic rationale for representation is established.

Employee involvement of a sort was fairly widespread in the early part of this century, though it was the employers who were the main initiating force in the establishment of pension schemes.[11] In some instances the involvement was restricted to consultation with staff representatives over the setting up of the scheme (foreshadowing the obligation laid upon employers by the 1975 Social Security Pensions Act to consult with recognised representatives on whether the scheme should be contracted in or out). Consultation might continue over the development or modification of the scheme, for instance by balloting over higher contributions. But there was also a distinct element of representation in the management committees or (more rarely) at trustee level. Colman's, Cadbury's and the majority of railway companies all had employee participation, generally with an employer majority but occasionally on a parity basis. However, as Hannah observes:

> ...it is not clear what this meant for the practical operation of the various schemes. The level of understanding of pensions was low, though interest in it occasionally rose to high levels. Information, except on the broad outlines, was probably not easy to come by. The Southwood Committee, which examined railway superannuation funds in 1909-10, expressed their surprise at the unsupervised nature of the funds, and recommended that annual accounts should be compulsory. However, pension funds in general remained regulated mainly by Trust Law for private statute. (1983, p. 33)

These issues persist, with concern still being expressed over the inadequacy of information, regulation and legal provision governing the funds. Participation has a long history, yet its objectives have remained ambiguous and its impact uncertain.

In the mid-1960s Lynes carried out a survey of employee participation in pension schemes. In the public sector he found that participation was prevalent, usually on a parity basis, but the picture was rather different in the private sector. Of the 100 largest companies in the UK, 54 replies covered 88 pension schemes, reflecting the strong tendency at the time to have separate staff and manual schemes. Including all forms of participation (on advisory councils as well as executive bodies), there was some form of employee representation in 41 of the schemes. In only half of these were the representatives elected, the others being appointed by management. Elected members were never in the majority. Representation was most common in long-established schemes and those which included both staff and manual workers: 'Companies starting pension schemes for the first time in the 1960s apparently did not feel the need to give their employees a voice in the administration of the schemes' (1969, p. 88).

This survey concentrated on advisory and executive bodies, rather than trustee boards and collective bargaining as we shall do. But Lynes noted that even in the schemes where participation was most strongly developed, 'the crucial question of the investment of the pension fund is not even dealt with by the management committee but by the investment manager and his advisers, who are responsible directly to trustees who are appointed by the company'. He concluded:

> It is surprising that the situation disclosed by this inquiry has been allowed to develop with so little comment or criticism. It would be interesting to know whether, with all the recent talk of democratic participation, the tendency for pension schemes to become still less democratic in the early 1960s has been reversed. (p. 89)

His cue was not taken, and the following decade saw little if any monitoring of developments.

In the next two chapters I attempt to fill this gap, tracing the growth of employee representation in contemporary pensions decision-making. Chapter 3 focusses on representation through the machinery of collective bargaining, Chapter 4 on representation at trustee level. But these two forms are neither homogeneous in themselves, nor do they cover the full range of representative modes. In particular there is often a system of consultative committees in many schemes. The 1973 Social Security and 1975 Social Security Pensions Acts went some way towards systematising pension schemes, bringing them into a single broad framework. But individual schemes vary enormously, not only in their scope and generosity but also in their organisational structure and the levels at which representation occurs.[12] The variety of management forms is too great to be neatly summarised; instead I shall conclude this chapter by setting out a number of examples, modelled closely on actual case studies. This will at least illustrate the organisational diversity of approaches to participation.

A: The first type may be termed *benefit bargaining*. It is drawn from a multinational company in the engineering industry, with separate schemes for hourly paid and salaried staff. (It also has a bowler and a top-hat scheme, labels which combine anachronism with accuracy.) The management of pensions is characterised by the company's insistence on the one hand that they should be an integral part of the overall bargaining process (higher pensions mean lower wages or other benefits), and on the other hand its reservation to itself of the control of the fund. The argument is that since the company shoulders the commitment to pay pensions at a certain level, it should have responsibility for managing the assets in order to meet those commitments. The sole trustee for the funds is a bank, with no employee representation at this level. The actual investments are made by a number of banks, whose performance is closely monitored by a branch of the company's finance department. Recent improvements in performance are reported to have reduced the company's costs by about £2.5 million in a single year. Significantly, chief responsibility for pensions has been transferred recently to the finance department from the industrial relations department, reflecting the growing concern with the capital as opposed to welfare implications of pensions. Representation is virtually synonymous with collective bargaining. Employees are represented, through the unions, on the Pensions Management Committee of each scheme, but these are largely concerned with discretionary payments and the formal auditing of accounts.

B: The second type denotes the *integration of bargaining and participation*. It is exemplified by a large conglomerate dealing mainly in paper and publishing. As with the previous case, pensions are part of orthodox collective bargaining. In addition, however, there is parity representation on the trustee board. The employee representatives are all themselves members of the scheme, nominated by the unions and formally appointed by the company. There is, however, no claim that the full trustee board is directly responsible for investment decisions. This is the province of the Investment Advisory Committee, on which there is no employee representation. Nevertheless, investment policy can be discussed by the trustees who are furnished with full information. It is worth adding that the value of the fund in question is about 40 per cent greater than the quoted value of the company itself, prompting one management representative to wonder aloud which business they were in: paper and publishing, or financial management.

C: *Overlapping participation and bargaining* can be illustrated by another multinational: this time in the chemical industry. It has separate schemes for staff and hourly paid. In the hourly paid scheme, participation in its various forms is based firmly on union structures. Unlike the previous two types, there is no formal bargaining over pensions, but there are Standing Committees with equal representation, whose function is to generate pressure for more resources to be devoted to pensions. Arguably these committees are assuming something of a negotiating function. There is also equal representation on both trustee boards but, unlike Type B, the company discourages close contact between the trustees and the members of the Standing Committees. An Investment Sub-committee deals with the investment of both funds. It meets monthly (whereas the trustees meet quarterly), and is chaired by a forceful outside trustee who is reported to be little concerned with participation. Member trustees attend the Investment Sub-committee on a rotating basis, such that each member trustee participates in about two of the twelve monthly meetings annually.

D: The fourth type is *participation without bargaining*. It is represented by a paper manufacturing company which bears the paternalist stamp of its family origins. There is participation at several levels, including the trustee boards where three out of the seven trustees are employees. The trustee board has a separate Investment Committee on which there are two employee trustees and three company trustees. These do not attempt to lay down tight constraints on the investment professionals. The system has been lovingly fostered by the pensions manager, who is keen to keep pensions out of mainstream company decision-making. It is the inverse of the first type, in that participation occurs at all levels but bargaining is completely excluded and the pensions decisions are maintained as a separate operation; moreover, the main company's control over the fund's assets is relatively loose.

Four types do not make a typology, but they do indicate the range of management structures within which representation occurs. This chapter has stressed the haphazard way in which pensions policy has evolved, at state and corporate levels. The extent to which members of pension schemes have been allowed representation in the management of company schemes has been similarly uneven, so far as one can tell from the limited historical evidence available. We turn now to examine current practice in the two principal modes of representation – collective bargaining and participation in trustee boards.

Notes
1. The title of Chapter 6 of Hannah's book (1986) is an apt one: 'Accident and Design in the Evolution of Pensions'.
2. Reflecting on the 'politics of pensions', R.H.S. Crossman described how his speech at the 1955 Labour Party conference, which committed the party to an earnings-related national superannuation scheme, was based largely on a pamphlet from a group at the London School of Economics which he had been given only the night before; in the same lecture he revealed that he had hoped that the contracting-out system for occupational pensions would last only for ten years or so by which time most private schemes would have come into the state system (1972, pp. 12, 21).
3. Retirement age on *Animal Farm* was yet another source of dispute between the two old war-horses, Snowball and Napoleon: 'Even when it was resolved – a thing no one would object to in itself – to set aside a small paddock behind the orchard as a house of rest for animals who were past work, there was a stormy debate over the correct retiring age for each class of animal' (Orwell, 1945, p. 26).
4. Samuel Johnson's caustic definition of a pension as 'pay given to a state hireling for treason to his country' both affirms the link with public service and foreshadows the recognition of pensions as deferred wages.
5. The magnitude of 'fiscal privilege' has been analysed by Hills, bringing together pension schemes, mortgages, insurance policies and other forms of saving into a common framework. Having demonstrated that pension schemes are one of the most significant forms of fiscal privilege, he concludes:

> The pattern of fiscal discrimination described is arbitrary in its effects between people saving through different institutions, in different assets and at times of differing inflation...There seems no obvious reason why we should wish the deployment of personal savings to be controlled by a small number of possibly unadventurous financial institutions, and yet that is what the tax system has encouraged. (1984 p. 97)

We return to Hills' second point later.

6. In contrast, where a category of worker was regarded as easily replaceable, and therefore expendable, employment conditions could be specified so as to avoid any pension costs at all. The 'marriage bar', introduced in the nineteenth century in the Post Office and then in the Civil Service, forced women to give up their jobs if they married; part of the motive was to save the cost of paying them the pension they would have earned by staying on to retirement.
7. See, for example, Melling (1983). A particularly well documented case comes from the history of the big French department store, the Bon Marché. In the late nineteenth century, the provident fund and the pension fund '... formed the capstone of the Boucicauts' paternalistic plans and of all the programs they established were the most extensively praised. Their benefits were substantial. The employee who remained with the firm for twenty years or more could expect to depart with at least several thousand francs from his provident fund account and a pension ranging from 600 to 1,500 francs a year. Yet the funds were also primed with effective mechanisms for shaping and controlling the workforce and for integrating them into the House.' (Miller 1981, pp. 100-101).
8. This and the following two quotations are cited in Green, 1982 (pp. 271-2). In the US we find the same use as an anti-strike instrument. Pension schemes were established in the late nineteenth century, primarily in businesses such as railroads or banks which faced labour unrest or were concerned about the stability of their workers. In 1915 the Grand Trunk Railway Company issued an ultimatum to its striking workers: come back to work or lose all your benefits. It also threatened to recall its retired wage earners to do the strikers' jobs. (Haber, 1978)
9. But not, it seems, extinct. Following the year-long miners' strike in 1984-85, the National Coal Board sought ways to avoid paying the pension fund credits for miners who supported the strike, despite advice from the Attorney-General that members of the mineworkers' scheme were entitled to credits for the year.
10. The guide to good practice on member participation issued by the National Association of Pension Funds in 1982 skated round the question of whether participation derives its justification in principle from the recognition of pensions as deferred pay. But it makes a general statement about the case for participation across all schemes: 'Pension schemes exist to provide benefits for members and their dependents. It is therefore logical and reasonable, whether the scheme is contributory or non-contributory, that members should participate in the operation of the schemes' (NAPF, 1982, p. 4).
11. Workers had early experience of scheme management through their own provident funds, set up to cover sickness and unemployment as well as old age. But these declined steadily throughout the first decades of the century, as employers set up their own schemes to supplement state pensions and trade unions shifted their attention to negotiating pensions. (Hannah, 1986, pp. 31-2).
12. In the public service, for example, which has the longest-established schemes and where participation outside collective bargaining also has a long tradition, pensions are a non-negotiable item dealt with by statutory regulation, and there is 'a veritable hotch-potch' of pensions arrangements in terms of both funding and contribution systems (see Thomson and Beaumont, 1978, p. 42).

3 The Extension of Collective Bargaining[1]

Of the numerous conceptions of democracy at work referred to in Chapter 1, apparently the simplest is that which equates it directly with collective bargaining. The interests of capital and labour are promoted respectively by management and union representatives in the process of negotiation, and alternative forms of joint decision-making are superfluous or worse. Although this position most commonly goes along with a class-based view of industrial relations, the most explicit advocate was no class warrior. In *A New Approach to Industrial Democracy* (1960), Hugh Clegg portrayed decision-making in industry as a quasi-parliamentary process. The role of trade unions is to act as opposition, legitimately putting their case against the ruling party; they should not seek to involve themselves in the task of management. Industrial democracy is achieved by the very pressure of a trade union movement in this oppositional role. This approach has been widely criticised at the theoretical level (see, for example, Blumberg, 1968). Above all, it is difficult to see how a system which dooms one 'party' to sit forever on the opposition benches without even the opportunity of crossing the floor to assume power has much claim to the title of democracy, even in diluted form. But Clegg's position is mirrored by writers from a very different political perspective, who see involvement in any form of participation other than collective bargaining as at best a foolish waste of time and at worst class treachery, so long as capitalism prevails. This view found forceful articulation at the time of the Bullock Committee, its proponents rejecting participation at board level as the height of misguidedness.

This supposed opposition – between collective bargaining and all other forms of participation – is a striking example of what Branko Horvat has termed a 'false antinomy' (1982, p. 22). It is true that collective bargaining may often be the most appropriate mode of interest representation and the most effective way of reaching decisions at work, including those governing the distribution of wealth. It is also true that collective bargaining may be weakened, deliberately or not, by the emergence of parallel participative initiatives. But there is no logical necessity that this should be the case, and empirically the evidence is very mixed. Furthermore, to counterpose bargaining and participation implies that the two are clearly distinguishable from each other. This is simply not the case, as pensions neatly illustrate.

Unemployment and hostile legislation have placed new constraints on labour's bargaining strength and eroded positions which seemed secure. They have exposed internal structural weaknesses and a loss of legitimacy within individual unions and the union movement as a whole.[2] The problems of maintaining solidarity are exacerbated by the haphazard way in which unions have developed (often engaging in unfraternal rivalry for members) and by uncertainty over whether they should take the American route of business unionism, adopt a high political profile closer to the more ideological lines of European unions, or simply stick with tradition. Yet the extension of collective bargaining is central to workplace democracy, at least within the British tradition. The evolution of bargaining, substantively and procedurally, has historically been the strongest force shifting the frontiers of control from unilateral managerial control to some degree of joint regulation. Over several decades, more and more issues which had previously been a matter of unilateral management decision were brought within the ambit of collective bargaining. Frequently this occurred informally at first, with custom and practice being consolidated later into formal procedure. From recognising the basic right of employees to be collectively represented over wage levels, employers – gradually, and with varying degrees of resistance – found themselves negotiating over such issues as manning levels, hours of work and a host of fringe and not-so-fringe benefits. In one sense, of course, these are all part of what has been called the effort bargain (Baldamus, 1961). But in addition to expanding the content and complexity of the bargaining agenda, the extension has also had ideological significance as an encroachment on managerial prerogatives. Even if in a given instance the outcome of negotiation is wholly unsatisfactory for labour, the fact that it occurs at all suggests that certain rights of joint determination have been recognised.

Chapter 2 referred to the evolution of pensions from gratuity to deferred wage. Since wages are the fundamental negotiating issue, it seems logical that this evolution should have been accompanied by the progressive inclusion of pensions in the negotiating agenda. If it is proper to bargain over pay, it hardly matters whether it is current or deferred. Reddin boldly suggests that the logic should be extended to cover all forms of remuneration:

> Is there even a clear primary (wage)/fringe (benefit) distinction? ... Trade union negotiators and employers are increasingly likely to negotiate wage settlements as part of a 'total remuneration' or 'quantum' approach. If an agreed sum is available, the negotiations determine the most effective division of the sum between wages, pension fund contributions, canteen prices and returfing the works

sports ground. Within this framework all benefits are wages by another name – *deferred wages* – although their distribution now becomes more complex. (1982, pp. 140-1)

Pensions are indeed being integrated into collective bargaining, but this chapter will illustrate the uncertainty and incoherence of the process. The logic of the deferred pay case has not always been followed. Pensions negotiations are to some extent *sui generis*, exhibiting characteristics that other issues do not have, and they present particular dilemmas to both management and unions.

To Bargain or Not To Bargain?
There have been two main lines of argument against the idea that pensions be included, in principle at least, in the negotiation process. It might be considered inappropriate to do so, or they might be considered insignificant as an item. Both arguments have been in evidence, and not only from managerial quarters.

In the first place, occupational pensions were originally very restricted in their spread, available mainly to government employees only. Just before the Second World War the small proportion of the workforce covered by pension schemes was mostly to be found in white-collar and managerial positions, where unionisation was virtually unknown. In the immediate post-war period it was only in the nationalised industries that there was extensive coverage for manual grades. In general, union efforts were concentrated on the improvement of state pensions – in so far as pensions were the focus of attention at all. It was only in the 1970s that the TUC and individual unions began to concern themselves actively with such issues as preservation of private pensions, index-linking of benefits in the public sector, removal of sex discrimination and disclosure of information (Green, 1982, p. 275). This lack of bargaining interest is recalled by a former General Secretary of the TUC: ' I can remember trying to get our TUC committees to take a more active view of unions negotiating pension schemes, being rapped over the knuckles for what was regarded as an attempt to distract attention from the real job of unions' (Len Murray, quoted in Moher, 1979).[3] On the union side, therefore, pensions were regarded as inappropriate as a bargaining issue because it was the state's responsibility to provide for people in their old age, rather than allow them to be dependent on their employer; but they were anyway regarded as insignificant compared with the more immediate task of improving wages in the pocket.

Today unions are far from having resolved the ambiguities of their approach. Formally they remain committed to state provision on a universal basis, but it is uncertain whether this implies actual opposition to private occupation-based provision, or simply a preference for relying mainly on a public welfare system. In practice, there are very few objections to be heard to the principle of company-based schemes. There is a degree of parallelism between these and company-based schemes offering access to private medicine, about which there is considerable controversy and internal division. Some unions see their responsibility as securing the most advantageous deal for their members irrespective of the broader implications for the relative quality of public and private health provision. They have little time for labour's supposed ideology of antipathy to profit being made from health care. On the other side are those who argue that agreements which include the payment of private medical insurance as part of the overall bargaining package will hasten the erosion of the National Health Service and foster the development of a divisive and inequitable two-tier system. Although similar arguments might have been deployed in the past in relation to occupational pensions, it is hard to see them developing much impetus today. If anything, the reverse: unions are tending to join with pensions management in defending the current occupational system against those who would dismantle it in favour of an individualised system of portable pensions. 'Privatisation' takes on a new meaning in this context, referring not to the transfer of service from the public to the private sector but to the breaking up of a corporate and collectively organised system.

The other uncertainty concerns the priority to be afforded to pensions as a bargaining issue, compared with other claims. To some extent, the relative sluggishness of union interest in pensions has been a reflection of longevity patterns: there is little point in trading off present income against future benefits if most of your members die before they have had much chance to enjoy these benefits. Class differentials still operate as manual workers die significantly earlier, so that the deferment of gratification implied in giving priority to pensions may seem less than seductive as a path to follow. In addition, income levels must rise above a certain minimum – again defined in relative terms – before the question of spreading it over time becomes even theoretically pertinent. Even if both these conditions are fulfilled – that workers should on average live long enough to give them a reasonable chance of drawing a pension, and that the margin of disposable income over a perceived minimum should be sufficient to allow the possibility of deferring a proportion of it – the question of priorities remains. In so far as a choice is involved, people may still opt for immediate gains rather than promised future ones.

Where pensions are accepted as a legitimate and substantive negotiating item, this does not necessarily mean that they are included in mainstream collective bargaining. Negotiators may seek to avoid a trade-off being made between pensions and wages or other benefits, if this seems to be the best way of maximising the total returns to labour. As one union official observed in the Glasgow study: 'We want to keep them separate from wage negotiations and to negotiate just over the level of contributions. If pensions would come into the regular wage claim, it would come bottom of the list.' (Changes in the level of contributions, of course, do have an immediate impact on the pay slip.)

So far the discussion has been phrased largely in the language of pure rational choice. It is consequently far from accounting for what actually happens. To it must be added a point which takes us closer to our concern with power and decision-making over pensions. The climate of negotiations is determined in part by the attitudes and behaviour of union officials. They are involved in defining the scope of the agenda, and in pursuing issues with different degrees of vigour and persistence. In general, unions might be expected to press, systematically or not, for an expansion of the bargaining process to include new items, and this is broadly true. But *pace* the sinister stereotype purveyed by much of the popular press, union officials are not for the most part Machiavellian manipulators of a mute membership. Their legitimacy and often their actual positions as representatives depend on their being adequately responsive to members' aspirations, whether or not these are explicitly articulated. For negotiators at all levels, pensions bargaining presents a particular problem. For most people, pensions is not an immediately relevant issue since retirement is many years off. Even if they are quite conscious of their eventual status as pensioners, the benefit is not an immediately tangible one. In so far as the sum available for wages and all other benefits is regarded as finite, if elastic, the 'better' the pensions deal the less scope there is for other forms of remuneration. Negotiators are aware that the preferences of members tend to be for earlier rather than later rewards, and there is unlikely to be substantial pressure on them to push hard for pensions – or as much 'reward' for them as negotiators in having secured a good pensions deal. The Glasgow research uncovered hardly a single instance of industrial action being taken over pensions; as one negotiator explained: 'Members won't take industrial action. I know they won't take industrial action. The employers know they won't take industrial action, and worst of all they know that I know they won't.' The temporal gap between bargaining effort and reward (for members and their representatives) affects the priority given to it.

There is a second factor which makes general union attitudes to pensions bargaining ambiguous. Where they are negotiated, pensions are almost invariably centrally negotiated. The broader implications of this are discussed later. But for shop stewards negotiating at local level pensions are not an issue on which they can achieve very much. And if a package agreed at central level involves a substantial pensions component, the scope left for bargaining over typically local issues such as shift premiums or bonus rates is correspondingly reduced. As Crouch observes of wider union goals in general (but citing pensions as an example): '... no gains from such demands are experienced in a manner which enables workers to make a direct connection between union action and outcome' (1982, p. 215).

In short, there are two reasons why negotiators might not give pensions high priority. There is the *temporal* one, that members' eyes tend to be fixed more on the short than the long term, and the 'political' kudos to be won from successful negotiations are lower when the benefits are not immediately tangible. And there is the *structural* one, that pensions negotiations take place at central rather than local level, so that the majority of union representatives – shop stewards at local or plant level – are not involved and therefore have little incentive to build up any head of steam on the issue.

Equivalent ambiguities exist on the employer's side, sometimes mirroring those of the unions and sometimes of a different kind. As long as pensions could be portrayed as a gratuity, there was no need to offer any form of negotiation over them. Even though few employers would today be bold enough to call pensions a gratuity, there are many who resist the inclusion of pensions along with pay and other items in the bargaining process. The most common strategy is to foster the feeling that pensions are an integrative rather than a distributive issue; in other words, that employers and employees have a common interest in improving pensions and there is therefore no place for bargaining with its inherent implication of an opposition of interest. The parallel is sometimes drawn with health and safety affairs: employees obviously want a healthy working environment, employers want not only a contented but also a fit workforce so there is coincidence of interest and antagonistic bargaining is inappropriate. The argument is correct in that the distributive aspect is not as dominant as it is with wages. There is indeed a greater measure of common interest. But it has been consistently shown how contentious many health and safety issues are, both in their financial implications and in the extent to which they affect the distribution of control at work (Schuller, 1985, Chapter 6). For our purposes, we need only note that the parallel is suggestive but inexact: health and safety is concerned primarily with the current workforce as workers, whereas pensions relate to them as ex-workers. The existence of contented pensioners affects the employing organisation only in so far as their satisfaction percolates back to and affects the attitudes of current employees.

The establishment of the deferred pay principle should be enough to dispel the 'common interest' argument in its naive form. Many employers, indeed, have taken the diametrically opposite direction, insisting that pensions are made an integral part of any negotiated agreement. In a handbook written primarily for employers, two members of the pensions industry observed that:

Of all the changes that have occurred since the publication of our first book on pension schemes in 1960, none is more noticeable than the increasing involvement and interest displayed by trade unions in pension schemes and by pension fund managers and consultants in trade unions. This trend is all to the good and, in the opinion of many, has taken far too long to cross the Atlantic. (Pilch and Wood, 1979, p. 187)

They list several disadvantages to the employer of including pensions in negotiations: the possibility of 'unrealistic claims', the chance that long-term prospects may be compromised by short-term concessions, and the problem of who is to represent the pensioners. But they also argue that to include pensions gives greater visibility to their costs and allows them to be traded off against improvements in other areas, whether these are pay items or fringe benefits. By 1979 average annual contributions in the private sector amounted to roughly £750 per member, and total annual contributions had risen from £500 million in 1956 to £9 billion in 1979 – more than three times as much in real terms. The normal employer contribution has now risen to over 12 per cent of annual salary. One survey of 20 UK and 20 US companies showed the former having an average pre-tax income of £65 million, of which an average £13.5 million – 20.8 per cent – was paid over in pension scheme contributions; the equivalent figures for the US companies were $133 million, and $14.2 million (10.6 per cent) (Fanning, 1983).[4] Even in the latter case, pensions clearly figures as a major item in corporate costs, and one to which employers are increasingly alert. It is of obvious advantage to employers to include these figures in the overall pay calculations – indeed, they would be foolish to ignore it.

On the other hand, some employers resist the inclusion of pensions on the grounds (usually left implicit) that it would entail ceding another area of decision-making to joint regulation. They may prefer to retain unilateral control, even at the possible expense of pensions being treated as a separate and additional item of labour costs – though they may, of course, attempt a dual strategy of maintaining pensions as a separate issue not subject to negotiation whilst at the same time including them as a cost item when it comes to wage negotiations.

However, it would as usual be a mistake to imply, by talking of employer strategies, that there is in every case a cohesive and rational management plan to minimise labour costs. In the first place the cost implications of many pensions agreements, especially those entered into in the mid-1970s, were not fully worked out. Eager to find ways round an incomes policy, and relying on the fact that pensions promises take time to come home to roost, some managements made offers with little regard for the long term. Parallel with the union representatives' problems in convincing their members of the substance of a temporally distant benefit, we find a management problem of integrating the various components of overall labour costs into a single coherent temporal framework.

A second incoherence arises from the division of managerial labour. Managers whose primary function is to control production costs may resist the setting up of a pension scheme in the first place or the improvement of benefits where one already exists. This generates tensions with their counterparts on the personnel side, including the pensions manager where such a management function is separately established. In a broad sense, the prime allegiance of managers as a class may be to the company rather than the workforce, but their behaviour and values cannot all be simply explained in these terms.

Just as local shop stewards gain little (in their representative status) even from advantageous agreements if they are concluded centrally, so pensions managers under certain company systems have little material or other incentive to minimise costs. They may give the welfare side of management a higher priority than those directly concerned with financial control. In such cases, efforts are made to resist the integration of pensions into the total remuneration package, if the pensions manager feels that he is more likely to achieve his own objective of a satisfactory welfare system. Alternatively, he may simply be more concerned to preserve his own empire than to serve any higher-order notions of economic efficiency, either in the sense of serving shareholders by minimising labour's share, or in the sense of improving employee welfare by effective management of the resources available.

The Form of Negotiation

Such is the background to the soft-shoe shuffle of pensions on to the bargaining stage. There are two main difficulties in tracing this path with any degree of precision (see Hyman and Schuller, 1984 for further detail).

The first is the lack of benchmark studies. It is only relatively recently that pensions have come to be recognised as a defined element of pay, open in principle to negotiation in the same fashion as other elements of the remuneration package. Although Clegg (1979) is probably correct to observe that the Social Security Pensions Act of 1975 has led to widespread bargaining over occupational pension schemes, he offers no evidence on this score. Brown's wide-ranging survey of British industrial relations, carried out at a time (1977-78) when pension schemes were burgeoning because of the limitations placed by incomes policy on direct pay bargaining, includes nothing about pensions negotiations (1981). Marsh's survey of industrial relations in manufacturing industry, published in 1982, also makes no mention of pensions. Even surveys specifically concerned with monitoring developments in pensions, such as those conducted every four years by the Government Actuary and annually by the National Association of Pension Funds, do not discuss bargaining as a means of determining benefit levels. It is only in the 1983 survey of industrial relations carried out by Daniel and Millward that pensions are specifically identified as an issue subject to collective bargaining.

Naturally the issue has not been wholly ignored where studies have been able to probe in greater detail. Three surveys carried out independently of each other in 1981 provide information. Two had samples of the same size (48 companies), one on a nationwide basis, the other in Scotland. The first (IRRR, 1981) reported that negotiations were carried out on pensions in one-third of the sample. The second reported divergent answers from different respondents within the same company: more than one in five senior union representatives considered that negotiations occurred, compared with only 4 per cent of senior managers (Cressey, Eldridge, MacInnes and Norris, 1981). The third survey was conducted by the CBI and covered 413 companies, of whom 15 per cent reported negotiations (CBI, 1981).

In the CBI survey, nearly half of the companies (46 per cent) also reported consultation over pensions. This explains the divergence revealed in the Scottish survey, and furnishes the second reason why it is difficult to judge precisely how far collective bargaining has been extended to include pensions. It is often the case that union representatives consider themselves to be involved in bargaining whereas managers see the same process as a consultative one. There are two factors involved here. First, there simply is no recognised set of characteristics which can be used to categorise a given exchange between management and union safely and definitively as either consultation or negotiation. Secondly, the process of categorisation, or attempted categorisation, is itself not an objective one. Because consultation implies no more than that the views of employees should have been sought and listened to before a decision is taken, management will tend to prefer it as a label for any exchange. Unions, on the other hand, will on the whole attempt to establish the right, at least in principle, to negotiate over a given issue. This may not be because they will immediately win substantive gains, but once bargaining rights have been established prospects for future gains may be rosier. Conversely, management may concede rather more through a consultative arrangement than they might have done otherwise in order to prevent pressure building up to transform the process into negotiation. Both the blurring of the boundaries and the motivations behind it are well illustrated by a practical management guide on the topic:

Topics outside, or not formally within the sphere of established collective bargaining, may subsequently become negotiable. Employers from time to time respond to suggestions of improvement made through consultative rather than negotiating channels, perhaps because of the strength of the case, or in preference to conceding bargaining rights formally. (Andrews-Jones and Churchill, 1983)

Daniel and Millward also report a degree of uncertainty about what is meant by 'negotiation', though they find in general quite a high degree of agreement between union and management respondents over what is and is not negotiated. They report that pensions are included in negotiations for 76 per cent of manual workers and 84 per cent of non-manual workers (1983, p. 197). This seems on the high side, given the relative newness of pensions to the bargaining scene (stressed by the Equal Opportunities Commission survey's account of union attitudes and practice, McGoldrick, 1984, p. 106). But it certainly shows that the practice of bargaining is now extensive.

From now on I shall draw substantially on the Glasgow research. This consisted of three main components: 2 extensive postal surveys (one of pensions managers and one of member trustees) and 18 case studies of organisations, all with some form of member participation and covering between them over 1 million members and assets of over £15 billion. Details of the research approach and the sample sizes on which the tables in this book are based are provided in the Appendix. The results presented below confirm that there is a substantial incidence of negotiation.

The surveys excluded very small schemes, and since union recognition is associated with size these are less likely to have bargaining arrangements in general, and *a fortiori* on pensions. Moreover, the member trustee survey was carried out through a number of trade unions, for reasons explained in the appendix, and the respondents in this component are therefore more likely than the average pensions representative to have some bargaining role. Nevertheless, almost three-quarters (72 per cent) of the member trustees who replied to the question on negotiations reported that negotiations occur on pensions and most referred to the existence within their organisations of a negotiating committee which dealt with pensions. In line with the discussion above, the incidence of reported negotiations drops when we turn to the managers' responses: less than one third (32 per cent) of the total report negotiations, though this rises to 45 per cent if only those recognising trade unions - that is where pensions bargaining is possible - are included. (It should be remembered that pensions managers may not be involved in negotiations even when they do occur). On a very rough, split-the-difference basis, we can conclude that orthodox negotiations over pensions certainly occur in well over half of the organisations included in the surveys. There is enough evidence to confirm the judgement of one leading firm of chartered accountants which sums up the calculations to be made:

> Effectively the value of the difference between the benefits which are received and the contributions which the employee makes represents an addition to the employee's remuneration. It is not surprising, therefore, that the scales of benefits to be provided under an occupational pension scheme and the division of the cost of providing those benefits between the employer and the employee are increasingly becoming a matter for negotiation. (Coopers & Lybrand, 1982, p. 8).

To supplement this, we can observe that consultation over pensions is widespread, reported in almost 60 per cent of the member survey. Naturally many of the arrangements are straightforwardly consultative without even a hint of negotiation. But once employee representatives are involved in consultative arrangements governing the administration of the scheme, it becomes difficult to segregate issues tidily into separate categories:

> The distinction between day-to-day management of pension schemes and collective bargaining for pension improvements is well understood in theory, but may not be clear-cut in practice. In theory it is simple enough to separate responsibility for administration from decisions involving changes in benefit and contribution scales. In practice, the two may overlap as where pensions are augmented or changes made in contribution rates following actuarial reports revealing surpluses or deficiencies. (Pilch and Wood, 1979, p. 189)

How the dividing line can be deliberately blurred is illustrated by the remark of a union representative in one of the case studies:

> We wanted to bring pensions into the bargaining system – the pensions advisory committees are the one piece of machinery outside collective bargaining. Once we realised we couldn't bring the committees in, we moved and captured them. The advisory committees are not quite as tame as the company thought they would be – though we don't publicise this, because it is outside the union system.

Allowing for the fact that the speaker is a full-time officer, who would therefore be expected to exhibit a degree of strategic awareness, and for an element of bravado in his comment, one can reasonably look on consultative arrangements in many cases as embryonic bargaining structures, (though like embryos they may never reach maturity, nor is the genetic development anything like as structured as the metaphor implies).

Further evidence for the interpenetration of bargaining and non-bargaining modes of representation comes from inspection of the *content* of pensions decision-making. Both managers and member representatives reported that the most common bargaining topics are benefit levels, contributions and increases in pension payments. This is wholly predictable, given that the motor force behind the inclusion of the issue in the bargaining agenda is the recognition of pensions as deferred pay. Occasionally more technical aspects such as the accrual rate also figured. Negotiations at present focus almost exclusively on how much individuals pay and receive, and not on broader strategic questions of fund management. The same items (benefits and contributions) are at the forefront of consultations, again as reported by both management and member representatives. There is an interesting further twist supplied by the managers' responses. After benefits and contributions, they report that the most common negotiating topic is the decision whether or not to contract out of the state scheme. Yet the Social Security Pensions Act imposed an obligation on employers to consult, not negotiate, with recognised trade unions. The probable conclusion to be drawn is that management view the presence of a legal obligation as imposing a stronger constraint on them than voluntary consultative arrangements do, and therefore regard it as more or less the equivalent of negotiation.[5]

The links between consultation and negotiation can be further explored if we turn to the trustees themselves. The trustee board is indubitably not a bargaining forum. Quite apart from the formal legal constraints, the ethos subscribed to by the vast majority of management and member trustees alike is not one of negotiation. Even should discussions become sharper in tone and the consensual atmosphere be dissipated, it is very unlikely that the boards could ever accommodate collective bargaining in the normal sense. Nevertheless, there is a degree of overlap between the functions of trustees and negotiators which cannot be ignored. In the first place, many member trustees have substantial experience as union representatives, whether as shop stewards, convenors, health and safety representatives, or as full-time union officials. This in itself is no more than suggestive: some trustees deliberately remove themselves from other union posts once they become trustees in order to prevent any perceived conflict of role, and the mere fact that an individual has held a union position certainly does not mean that he or she is inclined to treat the board as a place where negotiations take place. But member trustees are often in close and regular contact with other trade union representatives, both from their own union and from other unions. Two out of three member trustees in the sample met with representatives of the same union and two out of five maintained some degree of inter-union links. Meetings also took place with full-time officers or union pensions advisors. Links with head office were strengthened by the supply of information: 80 per cent of member trustees reported that they receive policy information from their union on a regular or occasional basis, and many of these regularly discuss the recommendations with their workplace negotiators.

The link between collective bargaining and representation at trustee level is not confined to trustees' membership of a union network. It will be thrown into sharper relief over the question of how fund surpluses are to be handled. Many funds have recently accumulated huge surpluses. High interest rates and stock market returns have greatly increased their assets, and their pension liabilities have often been simultaneously reduced because of substantial reductions in the company's workforce. As a result, surpluses exist which amount to millions of pounds, and the question is how and by whom, these surpluses are to be handled. Can employers simply take them back, directly or by reducing their contributions in the future? Or are they to be distributed to the members of the scheme, again either immediately or by reducing employee contributions?

In the US the practice of 'asset reversion' is already well developed, with companies clawing back more than $1 billion from their pension funds in 1984. In the UK the problem is more recent. In 1982 James Neill, a tool manufacturing company, transferred the entire certified surplus of the pension scheme – £2 million – from the scheme to the company's account. In 1984 another machine tool maker, B. Elliot, similarly transferred £5.5 million, equivalent to more than half its current stock market valuation. Early in 1985 Gomme Holdings revealed that its most recent actuarial valuation showed a £4.1 million surplus in the fund. The company announced its intention of clawing back £2.9 million of this (the rest to be distributed to scheme members), but this was rejected by the Inland Revenue. The Government was prompted to warn companies against asset-stripping pension schemes. At present the Superannuation Funds Office expects pension schemes to solve the embarrassment of surplus funds by improving benefits and reducing employer and employee contributions before any refund is made to the company. But the more that surpluses of these dimensions occur, the more difficult it becomes to treat the matter in this way (Dobie, 1985). Very awkward problems are presented to trustees and employers as to who should decide on the allocation of the surplus, and how. The dividing line between trusteeship and negotiation comes under severe strain at this point.

The occurrence of mergers and takeovers can also place member trustees in a very delicate position. They may find, while the takeover or merger is being discussed, that they are in possession of information which could have a substantial impact on the nature of the deal, or indeed on whether the deal goes through at all. The information may relate not only to the balance of assets and liabilities of the companies involved, but also to the bargaining position of their union on future wage negotiations. They may find that a request to keep such sensitive information confidential conflicts with their views on what they should do as trade unions.[6] It is worth noting the parallel with the BSC worker directors in the British Steel Corporation, who were placed in a very difficult position because of their early knowledge of impending redundancies which they were constrained from passing on to their negotiating colleagues (Brannen *et al*, 1976). At the very least it must be said that the issue is not clear-cut.

The Distinctiveness of Pensions Bargaining

So far I have argued that alongside the participation at trustee level described in the previous chapter there is a significant incidence of overt collective bargaining, even if it is difficult to get a clear idea of the pace of its evolution, and that this is augmented by forms of consultation which are often closely akin to bargaining arrangements. Overall, then, pensions are coming more into the mainstream of collective bargaining. On the other hand there are features which mark them off from most other areas of negotiation, and suggest that they are unlikely to be completely integrated.

The first is the manner or *style* in which pensions bargaining is conducted. There is general agreement amongst both union and management representatives that pensions negotiations are carried out in a different atmosphere to most negotiations. Even where both sides recognise that distributive issues are involved, the atmosphere is more relaxed, with a greater emphasis on joint problem-solving. The distinction was described by one union official as follows: 'The very continuity of pensions bargaining often provides a management–union link when all else is going awry. You may be having a bloody great row about pay but the superannuation committee keeps meeting. Pensions bargaining provides a stabiliser.' His views are echoed, though with a slightly different tinge to the remarks, from the management side:

> Union officials, perhaps because pensions have no direct impact on what you take home in your pocket, come across as a most sensible and responsible body of individuals... Pensions are less contentious than general negotiations. They involve more consideration of what is

desirable than what is available. Consequently there is very rarely any table-thumping.

Bearing in mind the in-built tendency of management to attempt to impose a unitary framework on any form of exchange, we can identify a number of reasons for this distinctive style. There is the temporal disjunction between the argument being concluded and its effects being perceived by the beneficiaries. I referred to this earlier as one of the factors which tends to give pensions a relatively low priority for negotiations; the corollary of this is that it removes pressure for immediate and visible results. Negotiations tend to be more protracted than normal as a consequence of the need to reconcile a wide range of interests within the scheme's membership. Allied to this is the fact that pensions are both relatively new and complex as a bargaining item. Sometimes there is an inadequate or confused data base on which to calculate the full implications of a deal. This may be exacerbated by division of managerial responsibility and uncertainty whether pensions is primarily a finance or a welfare issue: the company treasurer wants to base decisions on a straightforward cost basis, whilst the industrial relations department takes a slightly 'softer' line. There are technical complexities involved which take some time for both sides to grasp, especially if they are shrouded in wreaths of professional mystique. Even where the formal negotiations are quickly executed, the preparations for them have often spanned several months of joint elaboration.

The second major feature is the fact that pensions bargaining generally takes place at a *central level*, regardless of the degree of decentralisation of bargaining over other issues. Although practice is not always rational, the level at which collective bargaining takes place is related to its subject-matter. Thus safety matters and plant-specific rules are best determined locally, and wages in relation to the labour market (though the scope of the market, local or national, is highly variable). Other issues, of which pensions are a prime example, are best treated on a company-wide basis because of the need for uniformity created by actuarial and administrative considerations (Weber, 1967). A 1974 CIR report on industrial relations in multi-plant companies differentiated the issues to be negotiated between two levels:

> Where there is multi-level bargaining for manual workers within a company, issues regarded as general to all plants, e.g. basic environmental matters, employment conditions, pensions, fringe benefits and redundancy policy are retained under group control while others, mainly pay issues, are treated as specific to particular plants, product groups or divisions. (CIR, 1974, p. 39)

It is worth noting that the report added: 'However, even in companies where group-wide negotiations take place, matters such as pensions or redundancy arrangements are often not regarded by management as negotiable.'

Reddin remarks on the extent to which many employment-based welfare systems in the UK are negotiated at a different level from wages: 'Within one company, pension benefits are often less differentiated than wages. One manual plant may contain twelve unions, twenty different trades and forty negotiated scales of pay, yet there is a common pension scheme for all' (1982, p. 148). Daniel and Millward (1983, p. 197) show the extent of the gap. Although pensions are reportedly subject to bargaining for 76 per cent of manual workers and 84 per cent of non-manuals, the bargaining is carried out at plant level in only 11 per cent and 6 per cent of the cases respectively. Even capital investment is more commonly bargained over than pensions at plant level.

The reason for this is largely administrative. Some companies have grown by agglomeration but have failed to consolidate the different pension schemes into one. As a result, they are faced not only with the usual technical problems engendered by actuarial complexities, but also by a massive administrative burden and by the costs of managing a string of separate funds, all with separate trust deeds attaching to them. It has therefore usually made sense at some point to bring them all together, even at the cost of improving the benefits of the worst-off. But the consequences of this process are not restricted to a straightforward administrative rationalisation.

Over the last decades, the process of conglomeration has given many British companies a curious Lego-like structure, with all sorts of accretions stuck on at odd angles. On the one hand, mergers and takeovers have led to a concentration of capital, based on financial centralisation without this necessarily being accompanied by any significant degree of technical or industrial concentration (Strinati, 1982, p. 58). On the other hand, there is a polarisation between the centrifugal tendency towards a devolution of bargaining functions down to local level, and the centripetal tendency of bureaucratisation and strengthened corporate control. Pensions are one of the few employment issues which cut across the whole organisation, often covering all grades of employee, and which are also negotiable.[7]

There are two implications for the distribution of power and control at work, with particular reference to bargaining power. The centralisation of pensions bargaining implies the existence of machinery for co-ordinating union activity at this level. The Bullock Report pointed to the general absence of such machinery and recommended the setting up of Joint Representation Committees for the purposes of setting in motion the election of worker directors. Whilst union collaboration over pension arrangements may in itself appear to management as a functional arrangement carrying few dangers with it, the mere existence of such machinery can be looked upon as a potential means of forging links between portions of the workforce who are segregated occupationally, geographically and by the negotiating structures which operate on other issues. So far there is little evidence that anything along these lines has occurred (and the potential for such joint action may be limited by the fragmented nature of the British union movement), but structurally the centralisation of pensions bargaining may point towards new patterns of labour organisation.

Secondly, we must return to the content of negotiation. The focus of this chapter has been on the inclusion of pensions contributions and benefits as an item of negotiation alongside pay and other distributive issues. Although trustees do have links with other union representatives, and with union head offices, there is little indication that they are acting as bargaining agents. But given the recent prominence of pension funds as capital owners it is not inconceivable that attempts will be made to adopt a more negotiating style towards their management, as unions perceive that their demands on a whole range of other areas, including pay, manning levels and even issues such as union recognition itself, are influenced by the activities of the funds. For the moment it is sufficient to record the reply of one pensions manager, uttered with a sense of foreboding: 'I have noted an increasing tendency for worker trustees to introduce a "them and us" attitude. This may be because more of them have now been trained by their unions. It could also be because there is less money around, so it is more difficult to keep everyone happy.'

The concentration of finance capital, observable both in the conglomeration of industry and the growth of financial institutions; the pressures and doubts generated by economic depression and long-term unemployment; and the gradual establishment of pensions as a centrally negotiated item: all these suggest a certain volatility in the character of pensions decision-making.

Notes

1. As its title indicates, this chapter concentrates on pensions negotiations. Readers who are interested only in the activities of trustee boards and the management of the funds may wish to move on to Chapter 4, though there are important links between negotiations and trustee boards (see pp. 48–50).
2. It is arguable, for instance, that the closed shop has been to some extent a double-edged weapon for trade unions: apparently a source of immense strength, it has also reduced the incentive for representatives to nurture loyalty and commitment amongst their members.
3. Compare this with the United States, where a legal judgement in 1948 made pension plans a mandatory subject of collective bargaining (Woodbury, 1983).
4. Fanning also cites the case of a company with assets valued at £700 million in

December 1979, when an actuarial valuation revealed an unfunded liability of a further £730 million which had to be met by an increase in company contributions amounting to 29 per cent of salary costs. He grossly exaggerates by presenting this as typical, but the importance of pensions as an item of corporate costs is graphically illustrated.
5. Alternatively they may simply have recognised that an obligation to consult can best be discharged through formal negotiation.
6. They will need to be particularly careful because of the laws on insider trading (TUC, 1982).
7. See, however, Batstone (1984) for recent evidence of a more general shift to company-level bargaining.

4 Economic Democracy: Member Representation on Trustee Boards

The extension of collective bargaining reaches into several areas of corporate decision-making other than pensions. Participation in boards of trustees, by contrast, is peculiar to pensions. In this chapter I shall first set this type of participation in context by comparing it with other forms of economic democracy, broadly defined as systems of capital ownership whose particular common characteristic is that they involve workers as owners, as well as sellers of their labour. Economic democracy in this sense is to be distinguished from the sorts of organisational rights and procedures embodied in other forms of industrial democracy such as worker directors or consultative committees, where ownership is not a central defining feature. I shall then describe the nature of trusteeship – what trustees actually do – and explain the growth of member representation on trustee boards over the last ten years or so.

The Framework of Economic Democracy
From one point of view, there is no distinction to be drawn between 'economic democracy' and other forms of industrial democracy.[1] At the level of general definitions this is perfectly legitimate, but there are forms of participation which derive their distinctiveness primarily from their economic *constitution*, whatever the impact is on output, efficiency or other indicators of performance. Schematically these may be divided into three categories (see Schuller, 1985, Chapter 4 for further details).

The first is individual *financial participation*, interpreted as some form of share distribution to employees of the company concerned. The common term is 'profit-sharing', though this in itself disguises the fact that a shift in ownership (however marginal) is involved, and not just the distribution of surplus revenue. Profit-sharing in the UK has a long history, beginning in the third quarter of the nineteenth century when schemes were introduced mainly in response to labour unrest and to head off incipient unionisation (Bristow, 1974). Since then there have been periodic renewals of interest in the idea, and it is currently enjoying one such revival. Prompted by substantial fiscal inducements, 367 companies in the UK had introduced deferred share trust profit-sharing and 255 savings-related share option schemes between 1978 and 1983 (IDS, 1984).

The motives behind the schemes are diverse, a mixture of the financial, the practical and the ideological. The strongest financial motive is fiscal inducement, which allows the capital gain received in the form of shares to escape from tax in degrees which vary according to the number of years the shares are retained by the individual. The practical motive operates at company level, where the hope is that profit-sharing will make employees identify themselves more closely with its economic objectives. At national level the ideological motive is more prominent, with profit-sharing intended to bolster the legitimacy of private share ownership as the mainstay of orthodox capitalism.[2]

Our main concern is with the impact on the distribution of power. Here it is clear that individual financial participation neither is intended to have nor has in practice any significant direct impact, either within the companies where it occurs or more generally. This is most evident in the US, where the stock distributed under profit-sharing schemes (known as ESOPs – Employee Share Ownership Plans) rarely even carry voting rights (Blasi, Mehrling and White, 1983). There is certainly no prospect that the amount of shares distributed will under present circumstances reach levels which impinge on company decision-making; as important as the actual proportion is the fact that employees hold them on an individual basis, with no means of translating this into a collective say. There may, therefore, be material benefits for some employees from profit-sharing schemes but they are largely irrelevant to the internal control of companies.

Workers' co-operatives constitute a different level of economic democracy. They too have a long history (Thornley, 1981), also characterised by alternating periods of growth and decline but with a more persistent underlying continuity than profit-sharing schemes. Their significance for our purposes is that they represent a shift away from individual ownership, and especially away from external ownership of equity capital. Where money is raised from external sources it is characteristically on a loan basis, without this entailing a transfer of formal control to those providing the capital. This is at least the theory, though the experience of co-operatives reinforces the arguments rehearsed in the next chapter on the ambiguities of the link between ownership and control. Co-operatives come under pressure not only from market forces as they struggle to survive in a competitive – or pseudo-competitive – world, but also from other economic agents: banks who set the terms for their loans or suppliers who cause cash flow problems by pressing for unusually quick payment (Coates, 1976; Clarke, 1983).

As their name implies, co-operatives represent a form of collective financial participation. Ideologically they challenge the orthodoxy of financial individualism which asserts that people operate efficiently only as isolated agents looking after their own interests, whether as workers or capital-owners. Moreover, they can transcend to a degree the level of the individual organisation; in recognition of the vulnerability of single co-operatives, national and local agencies have been set up to provide a network of finance and expertise. The most prominent example of this is the famous Mondragon enterprise in northern Spain, where a whole range of co-operatives operate, buttressed by their own banking system, a network of training institutions to help provide new skills and, not least, a bonding sense of regional identity. The depth of democratic practice in the Mondragon co-operatives is still open to question (Thomas and Logan, 1982), but their economic performance is very respectable judged even on conventional criteria, and their record on other aspects such as the maintenance of employment levels is especially remarkable against a background of world recession. Of particular significance is the existence of a major financial institution, the Caja Laboral Popular (CLP), as an integral part of the co-operative set-up. The CLP is a credit co-operative which co-ordinates financial flows to the other co-operatives. It protects individual co-operatives from at least some of the difficulties which small firms often encounter, providing bulk purchasing facilities, marketing advice and educational programmes. It combines responsiveness to local economic needs with the discipline of financial expertise.

But the democratic impact of co-operatives – other than in the ideological sense referred to above – is largely limited to their own structures. This in itself is a constant subject of debate; ever since the Webbs' critical review (1921) they have been scrutinised for signs of 'organisational degeneracy' – in other words, how far they fail to sustain the original democratic form and spirit in which they were set up (Jones, 1980). For our purposes the significant fact is that by their very rationale they are inhibited from extending their influence beyond their own organisation. The exercise of external ownership rights conflicts directly with co-operative principles, so that they cannot legitimately acquire and use property rights over other enterprises. Their form of economic democracy is essentially limited to the particular units of capital which they themselves employ.

Since capital is not constrained by organisational, industrial or even national boundaries, we must look further for schemes which have equivalent scope. It is the structures which have at least the potential to extend beyond the confines of a single organisation that constitute the most wide-reaching form of economic democracy, and this is where participation in pension fund management is to be located. But it is not the only such form:

The concept of economic democracy is interpreted differently in different countries. In this report the concept is taken to be the one first introduced in Denmark. The term implies 'working towards a more equal distribution of incomes and wealth in society'. A consequence of this may be a change in the pattern of use in economic power...This would then pave the way towards furthering industrial democracy through economic democracy. (ETUI, 1983, p. 16)

The ETUI report then covers a number of ownership forms. Although it includes reference to individual financial participation schemes of the kind referred to above, it concentrates on forms of collective capital formation which exist, actually or on paper, in Austria, Denmark, France, Italy, the Netherlands, West Germany and Sweden. The common thread is that a part of the surplus created from profitable economic activity should be accumulated in funds which both belong to and are controlled by the workers who contributed to the creation of that surplus. The democratic character of such forms derives from one or more of the following: their ownership structure, the process by which they are governed and the use to which they are put.

In the industrialised countries the only scheme of significance which is both in existence and has been designed deliberately to promote economic democracy is the Swedish system of *wage-earner funds*. From their original conception, by the chief economist of the blue-collar union (LO) Rudolf Meidner, they have followed a tortuous and acrimonious path, including an election defeat for the Social Democrats in 1976 for which they were held by some to be largely responsible. The proposals finally reached the statute book in 1983, substantially mutated but still accompanied by an enormous display of hostility from the employees. The system is composed of five regional funds, made up by contributions from companies of 20 per cent of their profits above a certain level, and by a small proportion (0.2 per cent) of the wage bill. The contributions should initially (in 1984) amount to some 400 million Kronor annually for each fund, which they use to buy shares on the stock exchange. The level of capital formation is thus preserved or enhanced, without causing a further inequitable concentration of private wealth. The funds are required to invest in Swedish companies (including foreign-owned companies operating in Sweden), and are expected to concentrate on long-term investments. They are to be managed by boards of nine people appointed by the state, of whom at least five are to represent employee interests (Linton, 1985).

The funds have one other feature (not present in the original proposals) which links them even more closely to our present concern. They are to be administered within the framework of the Swedish National Pension Insurance Fund, and their boards are to operate in parallel to the four boards which manage that fund. The wage-earner funds are required to yield a real return of at least 3 per cent, which is transferred to the Pension Insurance Fund boards for distribution. In short, a structural link has been set up between the existing pension fund system and the new wage-earner funds.

The wage-earner fund system has been in operation too short a time for any assessment to be possible, but three points are worth making. First, the measures form part of a characteristically Swedish approach which ties them into other moves towards greater democracy at work, including the presence of worker representatives on company boards and the provision of professional advice and back-up services for these representatives. There is no illusion that one reform on its own can transform the pattern of industrial and financial control. Secondly, even in a country accustomed to a high degree of public intervention (though not, it is worth stressing, state ownership) and with a highly centralised system of collective bargaining, there have been major problems in achieving a coherent balanced structure for the funds whilst retaining at the same time a proper degree of democratic accountability. Thirdly, the significance of the initiative is as much ideological as practical. It is projected that by 1990 the funds will between them own a maximum of 5-6 per cent of Sweden's equity capital (and no one fund may own more than 8 per cent of a given company). This is considerably less than was originally envisaged, but the scheme represents a challenge to the whole system of capitalist property rights and the basis on which economic surplus is generated and distributed.

These three points form, in my view, the agenda for any contemporary discussion of the feasibility of wage-earner funds in other countries, including the UK.[3] But we can turn now to concrete evidence on an existing form of collective capital formation. Pension funds were not established to promote economic democracy and the idea that they should be used in that way is fiercely resisted in many quarters. But whereas the Swedish wage-earner funds have in the course of their gestation acquired attachment to the pension system, pension funds in the UK have – *post partum* as it were – developed features which are at least embryonically democratic, in the shape of member representation on trustee boards. Before examining this process we shall look at what the boards actually do, whether or not there is member representation on them.

Trusteeship

Commonly, 'trustee' conjures up the image of someone of benevolent disposition charitably occupying themselves with looking after a dead friend's assets, on behalf of a child or children. Historically, indeed, this was broadly the case, at least as far as the function (as distinct from the personality) of the trustee is concerned. The current debate about the adequacy of trust law is partly fuelled by doubts whether laws originally framed to deal with individual patrimonies are appropriate for huge blocks of collective saving.[4] It raises questions about how trustees come to hold their positions and what they actually do.

Trusteeship of pension schemes can take one of a number of different forms. The board of trustees may be constituted by individuals, each appointed as an individual named in the trust deed. Or a trustee company may be set up, independent of the main company, with directors as trustees. In either of these cases the option of participation is relatively straightforward (whether or not it actually occurs), with trustees elected by or selected from the membership. A third possibility is for a separate organisation such as a bank to be appointed as a corporate trustee, in which case it is very much more difficult for participation to occur – in pratice, only if powers are delegated to a Committee of Management. There are also schemes which have no trustees; the most important instance of this are local authorities which have instead a superannuation panel drawn mainly from elected councillors, who are not themselves members of the scheme. (Other public-service schemes such as the Civil Service have a so-called statutory trustee, which also means that direct member representation is excluded.) For the sake of simplicity, in what follows I shall refer to participation or representation on trustee boards, regardless of whether the body concerned is formally speaking a board of trustees or a trustee company.

The functions of the trustees are very loosely defined. The textbook definition of a trust, in all its legal glory, is 'an equitable obligation, binding a person (who is called a trustee) to deal with property over which he has control (which is called trust property) for the benefit of persons (who are called the beneficiaries) of whom he may himself be one and any one of whom may enforce the obligation'. (It is worth noting that the pronouns reflect present circumstances quite accurately; 94 per cent of the trustees in the Glasgow survey were male.) In true Anglo-Saxon tradition there is no formal codification of the law of trusts; one rather sanguine observer holds it to be 'that distillation of the wisdom of the judges over the centuries as relates to property held in a fiduciary capacity', concluding that 'it is perhaps a peculiar merit of the English legal system that in this, as in so many other sections of the law, no statutory intervention has been necessary' (Slattery, 1981, p.3). The distillation, however, is less than crystal clear. Fortunately there is no need to go into extensive technical detail on the legal position, though if the funds' management becomes more of a political issue the legal context will be the subject of intense interest (see Chapter 6). What does need to be sketched out at this juncture are the functions of trustees as they are practised. This must be prefaced by a strong caveat that trustees discharge their obligations in very different ways. Not only can they delegate a substantial amount of their powers, for example to a Committee of Management; but they vary widely in the attention they give to each of the possible functions and the extent to which they actively involve themselves in them.

This is not the same as saying that there is a great diversity of views over which of their functions is formally the most important. The vast majority regard the supervision of the assets as the most important of their duties, since to dissipate the assets would render the other functions more or less irrelevant. But the way in which this function is interpreted varies greatly, so that verbal uniformity covers diversity of practice. Moreover, although all trustees are under the same obligations, there is often an implicit division of labour within the board, with trustees informally assuming different roles. We shall need to distinguish between the functions of trustees as a collective body and the way individual trustees contribute to the operations of the board.

In short, trustees' time is allocated very variously between their several functions, both across and within boards. The position of the trustees reflects the broad division described in Chapter 1 (pp. 5-20): they are concerned with both the personal circumstances of individual pensions and future pensioners – the management of age – and the management of often very large sums of capital. The blending of these roles is not always a comfortable process. The third strand – that of democracy in management – is not formally woven into the functions of trustees, but there have been attempts to change the law in this direction; more significantly, participation is becoming established to a degree as normal practice, sanctioned by convention as well as philosophy.

The most pervasive feature of trusteeship is that it is supervisory. For almost all the functions outlined below trustees are concerned with ensuring that things are done properly, as distinct from doing them themselves. This distinction cannot always be maintained, but it is an important one of principle. In particular it places a good deal of significance on the relationship between the trustees and those who are employed actually to execute the management of the scheme and its assets. The trustees' first obligation on taking up appointment is to familiarise themselves with their duties and with the circumstances of the particular trust. They then occupy themselves with some or all of the following (subsequent chapters put more flesh on most of these bones, and the effect on them of member representation):

1. Management of the assets
The trustees' most important function is to ensure that the assets entrusted to them are properly invested. This function has two aspects: the supervision of *investment policy*, and the *monitoring of investment performance*. The former looks mainly to the future. Trustees may lay

down, with greater or less degrees of precision, the proportions of the funds to be invested in different areas: equities, gilts, property and other items (such as the antiques which gained the British Rail fund such notoriety). They may also specify how much is to be invested overseas, again in each of these areas (shares, government debt and so on). Their hands may be partly tied by trust deed, which can restrict investment of certain types. One of the commonest types of restraint is on the level of 'self-investment', where the scheme puts money back into the company by buying its shares. The restraint is designed to prevent an incestuous involvement which could mean, in the case of bankruptcy, that employees' pensions disappear along with their jobs.

Guidelines on investment policy do not need to be set as precise single figures. Instead they are likely to indicate a range or a maximum: 30-40 per cent of the fund to be held in equities, and not more than 10 per cent to be invested overseas, for example. Investment decisions mainly concern 'new money', the inflow into the fund from contributions and from existing investments; the trustees do not reshuffle the pack each time they meet (though the practice of 'churning' or unnecessary share-dealing by investment managers to earn higher commissions raises some pertinent questions).

Laying down these guidelines need not involve the trustees in individual decisions about particular investments. The money allocated to equities may go to the ICIs of this world or to smaller companies without the trustees being involved at this level at all. In practice, of course, there is a spread of investment within any given sector. One prominent criticism of the funds' collective behaviour is that they concentrate on larger companies, in which their investment managers feel safer and which can absorb substantial amounts of money at one go. The reply is made that it is not worthwhile spending time assessing investment outlets which even if they do look promising can only absorb a tiny fraction of the amount which has to be placed. The point here is simply that trustees do not normally participate in individual investment decisions. 'You don't buy a dog and bark yourself' as one pensions manager put it, in a rather uncomplimentary reference to investment advisers. In the Glasgow research we did interview one trustee who took pride in 'getting his shoes dirty' visiting the actual properties in which his fund invested; exactly how he weighs up the value of a particular premiss in a particular shopping precinct was not quite clear. Of course, potentially controversial decisions such as purchasing the shares of a company in the process of being privatised are another matter, but the number of such obviously contentious individual decisions is limited.

Monitoring fund performance means reviewing how well the investments have done in terms of yield. (For pension funds, given their long-term liabilities, the distinction between capital growth and income is largely irrelevant.) The trustees must ensure that the professionals have conformed to the guidelines which have been laid down. They must also satisfy themselves that within those guidelines a reasonable job has been done of achieving a return. This seems likely to be one of the most vexed areas of the future. The measurement of fund performance is an activity which inevitably requires a great deal of technical sophistication. Since the arrival of Mrs Thatcher's government we have been generally encouraged to think of economic management as family budgeting on a vastly magnified scale, presumably with gigantic Mr Micawbers as treasurers. But the returns to pension fund investments cannot be measured in such simple terms, matching earnings directly to the amount invested over a given period. In particular, account must be taken of the maturity of the scheme (that is the distribution of pensioners as against contributing members) and of the timescale of appraisal, as investments which appear to be poor in the short term may eventually yield a better return overall.[5] On the other hand, the technical complexity of measurement can be used, wittingly or not, to prevent trustees from grasping the underlying trend of performance. The TUC guide to trustees points out the following weaknesses of some of the performance measurement services used:

- the tendency for them to concentrate both managers' and trustees' minds too much on 'coming top' in the short term at the expense of the long term;
- the assumption that capital values as expressed by stock market prices are necessarily 'right';
- the failure to indicate the degrees of risk involved;
- the coyness about providing details of the turnover and activity within funds, which would show how much they are paying to managers who make a commission on each transaction. (TUC, 1984, pp. 59–60)

The problem is one of finding a balance between necessary reliance on professional expertise and adequate supervision of what is actually being done. Trustees cannot sit in peer judgement on investment advisers, but they have to be confident that what is done in their name is indeed beneficial to their members. The most contentious circumstance is likely to be when a trustee refers to a criterion which falls outside the professionals' sphere of experience and competence, and asks for measures to be built into the assessment which conventional accounting practices reject as irrelevant. More generally, there is the problem of the funds' broader obligations to ensure economic stability. In short, monitoring 'financial performance' is a problem whose technical character is surprisingly uncertain; it involves questions of what is to be measured as well as of how to measure it. The trustees' ideas of 'best interests' may be at variance with those of professionals brought up on the City code and accustomed to thinking chiefly of the short-run outcome of individual decisions. It is worth also noting that the ideas of the members may be at variance with both.

2. Appointment of management and advisory personnel

This function follows from the previous one. It is not one on which much time is at present spent by trustees, but it has a strategic significance nonetheless. In order to ensure that assets are properly invested and the scheme efficiently administered, trustees must be confident that the people responsible for these various functions are competent. The personnel involved include pensions administrators who handle the day-to-day aspects of management, ensuring that members get the benefits they are entitled to, are properly informed and so on; the investment managers, internal or external (principally stock brokers and merchant banks); property consultants; and the actuary who assesses the balance between the scheme's assets and liabilities. Until recently, most schemes had very little turnover in any of these capacities, and it would certainly hint at something of a scandal if trustees required the removal of an administrator. Once an actuary is appointed, he is likely to continue acting for that scheme as a matter of routine. The same used to be true of banks and other advisers. But as competition to manage the lucrative pension fund business hots up there is now a greater turnover of advisers, who have to be more aware of the need to demonstrate the quality of their services. The larger funds may have several banks advising them simultaneously, and either regularly or occasionally replace one, hoping to keep the others on their toes. Such alertness is by no means universal, but it does indicate some pressure towards greater accountability. The obligation to take this supervisory role seriously is emphasised by the TUC guide: 'Trustees need not simply take pot luck or assume that the terms offered [by advisers] are the only ones possible: they can bargain for a different arrangement, and negotiate between a number of different groups until they get precisely the service they want' (TUC, 1984, p. 48). Although the supervision of management personnel may not as yet be an active trustee function, it is not at all insignificant.

3. Rule supervision

It is worth reiterating at this point that trustees are not negotiators and the trustee board is not a bargaining forum. As we saw in the previous chapter, however, the dividing line between negotiation and other forms of participation is often blurred. Of all the functions of trustees, the supervision of scheme rules is probably the one that at present verges most closely on the negotiating arena. Trust deeds vary in their format and in the detail with which they specify the scheme's structure and content, but they usually fall into two parts. The Trust Clauses set out the powers and duties of the trustee, covering investments, alterations, transfers and winding-up requirements. The Rules Clauses outline the contributions and benefits payable, and usually also the discretionary powers to be exercised by trustees. The deed therefore commonly embodies rules which may have been arrived at through collective bargaining, and it is the trustees' duty to interpret these and supervise their implementation.

Trustees are legally required to be familiar with the rules, though once again the degree of familiarity which is accepted as adequate varies widely. Rules change, of course, and the process of amendment can (combined with the habitual legal jargon) produce an intimidatingly cumbersome document – so much so that the TUC guide (1984) finds it necessary to encourage trustees to insist on new deeds being produced to replace over-annotated and unmanageable scissors-and-paste concoctions. Quite apart from the growing importance of occupational pensions in people's planning for their future, the diversification of retirement patterns and the overall increased complexity of schemes mean that this apparently mundane function is likely to assume greater significance. As negotiators deal more regularly with changes and improvements to the scheme, and as fewer individuals follow wholly routine paths into retirement, so mastery of the rules becomes a demanding responsibility.

4. The provision of information
Information falls into two broad categories: that relating to the individual's personal circumstances and that relating to the scheme as a whole. In recent years the issue of information has begun to assume a higher profile for a number of reasons. First, more employees are faced with decisions about their future which involve – or should involve – knowing what their financial circumstances and options are. As early retirement and redundancy schemes proliferate, so the concern for better information increases, even amongst those who are not immediately affected. Secondly, more people want to know about how the funds are being used, both because it affects them personally and for reasons of a more general political or ethical kind. Thirdly, pressure for greater accountability has generated demands for more systematic and standardised forms of information provision. In a more general context, the current government has made information to employees a central part of its programme for employee involvement. In the case of pensions, information and participation have been particularly closely linked, with the Occupational Pensions Board regularly yoking them together (along with solvency) in its reports (for example OPB, 1975).

Again, trustees are likely to assume a more active role in the future. Some of the information to be provided is specified by law – for example the Employment Protection (Consolidation) Act of 1978 requires the employer to give a statement of his or her contract to an employee within thirteen weeks, containing details of any pension scheme. As far as the trustees themselves are concerned, the Superannuation Funds Office requires, as a condition of a scheme's approval under the Finance Act of 1970, that an employee should be informed of various benefits such as those payable on normal retirement or on death in service. The National Association of Pension Funds has issued a code of practice on information to members, and presents Golden Pen awards annually to virtuous practitioners. The TUC guide suggests the following as good practice: each member should automatically be given a booklet outlining the scheme, a personal benefit statement and a copy of the simplified annual report, and should have easily available on request the deed and rules, full audited accounts, the annual report and the latest actuarial valuation. Trustees are formally responsible for the policy practised on disclosure of information – how much information is to be available or distributed, and on what basis; they may also as individuals be active themselves in disseminating it.

5. *The exercise of discretionary powers*

Here too there is a distinction to be drawn between decisions dealing with a principle which will cover the majority of cases and those which require consideration of individual case histories. Discretionary powers are mainly exercised over death benefits, early retirements and early leavers. A typical case might deal with an 'unmarried widow', who has lived with an employee as his common law wife and feels after he dies that she is entitled to his continued pension as she would be if they had been legally married.

In some schemes, the pensions manager will handle the bulk of discretionary cases, with the trustees merely granting their formal approval. In others, trustees – or a sub-committee of them – will scrutinise the cases individually. Again there is a balance to be struck between reliance on professional judgement and adequate supervision of the interests of all members. 'It is important to make sure there is enough information to make a proper decision, but trustees need to balance this factor against a need to avoid delay, since the people concerned are quite likely to need the money urgently' (TUC, 1984, p. 86). The TUC guide goes on to stress that the trustees must act independently of the company, where for example a person is put forward for early retirement on the grounds of ill-health when the real reason is that he or she does not fit in with the reorganisation of a department.

From unmarried widows to bulk buying of government debt: it is clear from this outline of trustees' functions that they are in principle called on to cover a wide range of activities. The diversity of tasks appears intimidating. It fully reflects the intertwining of two of the strands identified in Chapter 1 and summarised as the management of age and the management of capital. We turn now to the third strand: the democratisation of management.

The Emergence of Member Trustees

Chapter 1 dealt at some length with the 1977 Bullock Report on worker directors. One reason was to allow a contrast between the reception – and fate – of the Bullock proposals with the emergence of employee representatives as members of the trustee boards of pension schemes. There are several significant differences between the two types of representation, some obvious, some less so, and I shall return to this in some detail in Chapter 7. The fact remains that at the same time as British industry was mounting a concerted attack on the idea of worker representatives sitting on company boards there was a substantial and uncontested shift in the composition of bodies endowed with formal decision-making powers over millions – in some cases billions – of pounds. There was, certainly, fierce resistance to the proposal of the 1976 White Paper (*Occupational Pension Schemes: The Role of Members in Running of Schemes*) that trustee representation should be mandatory and based on recognised trade unions. But this was nothing compared to the furore surrounding Bullock, and was often accompanied by a broad willingness to accept the principle of representation – and even equal representation – at trustee board level. The chief objections were to the idea of a mandatory legal requirement and to the proposal to base participation on the single channel of trade unions. The subsequent implementation of participation described below has taken place largely without fuss or friction.

One reason for this peacefulness is that a decade in the life of an institution such as a pension scheme is in some respects rather a short time, and the scope for an immediate and substantial impact by member trustees is correspondingly limited. Typically, trustee boards meet less frequently than company boards – usually on a quarterly rather than a monthly basis. Policy-making is rarely subject to dramatic swings or to the need for quick decisions. Although it is not only at the actual meetings that member trustees can make their presence felt, the pace of events tends to be slower in pensions than in other areas of corporate policy. It is important to bear this in mind when evaluating the experience so far and assessing the prospects for the future. But first the facts, as far as they are known.

In the vast majority of pension schemes, members have no direct representation at all in their management. The reason for this is often quite simple. They are small schemes, with only a few members and correspondingly limited assets. There is no point, as far as the company is concerned, in incurring the costs of administering the fund as a separate entity. The scheme is therefore either 'fully insured', that is it is handed over in its entirety to an insurance company which takes care of both assets and administration, or the insurance company takes on only the management of the assets. These can be handled as a separate unit, or pooled with those of a number of other clients on whose behalf the insurance company acts. In fully insured schemes there is only a very minor role potentially available for representatives of the scheme members, confined mainly to basic administration and occasional decisions on discretionary payments. 'Managed' schemes offer a little more potential in principle, but not much in practice. Of the 90 000 schemes in existence, the great majority fall into the category of 'insured scheme'. But these cover, even in aggregate, only a small proportion of all pension scheme members, and of total pension fund assets. Amongst the larger schemes the picture is somewhat different.[6]

Information about the composition of trustee boards is very scanty, a reflection in part of the generally low level of information released about the way schemes operate, and in part of the diversity of scheme forms, which makes it difficult to bring survey material together into coherent form. In the late 1970s the National Association of Pension Funds (NAPF) was actively discussing the possibility of issuing a code on member participation and conducted a special survey of its members. Of the 769 replies 52 per cent claimed some form of participation; of these 250 – just under a third of the total – had member participation in the trustee board only, and a further 31 had both participation of this kind and pensions negotiating committees (Cole, 1981). The NAPF includes a mention of participation in the annual survey it conducts, but given the complexity of management structures sketched out in Chapter 2, it requires a more extensive range of questions to give anything like an accurate idea of the extent of representation.

More details come from the Government Actuary, who publishes a report every four years on various aspects of pension schemes. His two most recent surveys, conducted in 1975 and 1979,[7] included questions on member participation, but it was only in the later one that a distinction was made between trustee boards and management committees. It covered 11 500 schemes, excluding the very small ones (under 30 members) in the private sector. (See Table 4.1).

The broad nature of the 1979 survey made it difficult to be certain about the constitution of the trustee boards and the Government Actuary acknowledges ambiguities in the responses. Nonetheless he points out that in over half of all the schemes surveyed, some of the

Economic Democracy: Member Representation on Trustee Boards 69

Table 4.1: 1979 Government Actuary survey on numbers of schemes and of members according to whether a representative of employees is a trustee

Status of representative	Private sector Schemes	Private sector Members (000s)	Public sector Members (000s)
Elected member(s)	400	900	350
Nominated member(s)	5000	2200	900
Some elected, some nominated	800	600	50
None elected or nominated	5000	1200	300
No trustees	300	100	3900

Source: Government Actuary's Department (1981), Table 13.3.

trustees are elected by the members of the scheme or nominated from amongst the members as their representatives. It is evident from Table 4.1 that the bulk of the 'representatives' are nominated, presumably by management. The report also provides some information on the methods of selecting representatives, but inevitably there is little flesh on the bones. Allowing for its particular emphasis, the comment of a report on equality of pensions treatment for men and women could be applied just as well to participation:

> Existing surveys, however, do not cover all relevant issues; they do not enquire beneath the organisational structure of schemes to shed light on interpretation and practice, particularly in the more delicate areas of scheme management. These include the use of discretionary powers, the responsibility for decisions, definitions of dependency, selection of beneficiaries, provisions during maternity and childcare leave, divorce and separation, and the treatment of common-law partners. (McGoldrick, 1984, p. 6)

From a different angle, one might expect trade union offices to be a source of information on the extent of participation, at least within the ranks of their own members. This would in any case yield only a partial picture, because even in companies which recognise unions for bargaining purposes pensions representation is often not based on union structures. But union records on this score are very patchy. The Glasgow member trustee survey was conducted directly through seven of the major unions: APEX, ASTMS, BIFU, EEPTU, GMWU, TGWU and USDAW (see Appendix). These are substantial organisations, in several cases with a particular, almost professional, interest in financial management and with an above-average level of service to their members on pensions matters. Yet they had no up-to-date record of where their members sit on trustee boards.

In short it is impossible to provide a comprehensive picture of representation at trustee level. Nevertheless, the results presented below confirm the Government Actuary's general outline and fill in some of the canvas. They also give a strong indication of the direction which events have taken over the last ten years or so. Before going further, we need a note on one point of terminology. How are the representatives on trustee boards to be designated? 'Employee participation' is the umbrella term which covers most forms of representation, and this suggests 'employee trustee' as the term for those participating on trustee boards. But not all employees are members of the pension scheme where one exists; unlike those employees who are not members of trade unions but benefit anyway from agreements negotiated by union representatives, employees outside the pension scheme could not be said to be represented even indirectly. It is also the case that some of the representatives are not employees of the organisation concerned, but full-time union officials. This does not necessarily impair their legitimacy, but it makes the designation 'employee' trustee doubly inappropriate. 'Member trustee' is open to the second of these reservations, but seems on balance the better choice.

Member trustees are, therefore, trustees whose place on the board is a function of their membership of the scheme or of their status as union representative, and not of their position in the organisation's management structure or of particular expertise. They arrive on the board through a variety of channels: appointment by management, election by members, nomination by unions and so on. So participation ranges from the most primitive level of a single member trustee nominated by management to a system in which a majority of trustees are elected by the members. Taking the simple incidence of participation first: there were member trustees of some description in 70 of the 131 schemes in the pensions manager survey which had trustees[8] – a basic level of participation of 54 per cent. Predictably, it occurs most commonly in the largest schemes: two-thirds of those with 5000 or more members have some degree of member trustee participation, compared with just over two-fifths of those with less than 5000. No differences emerged between contributory and non-contributory schemes, but only 15 of the latter figured in the survey (roughly in line with the proportion of non-contributory members in the population as a whole).

Of itself the mere incidence of participation is interesting but not very significant. Its significance is substantially increased if we take into account the *depth* of participation – that is the proportion of places filled on the trustee board by member trustees. Most trustee boards are quite small. Just under half (48 per cent) had between six and ten members and a further 40 per cent had less than that, so only about one board in eight had more than ten people sitting on it. (For curiosity's sake it may be worth recording one case of elephantiasis, with 30 trustees.) The actual meetings are likely to include more people as there will normally be a number of consultants and other personnel sitting in in an advisory capacity. But it is interesting to relate the total number of people involved as trustees to the amount of capital involved: the top 100 schemes in the UK have under 1000 trustees, responsible between them for about £70 billion – about £70 million per trustee.

If representation takes the form of a lone member trustee surrounded by management appointees, this must be distinguished from parity representation, where there are equal numbers of management and member representatives. Profiles of the boards can be built up by matching the number of member trustees against the total number of trustees. The results are shown in Table 4.2. From the table it can be seen that member trustees constituted exactly half of the trustee board in over one-quarter of the cases; altogether they formed more than two-fifths of the board in well over half of the cases. In only 11 per cent was their presence less than one-third. So even where they are a minority, they are a substantial minority. Once again, the degree of participation is far greatest in the largest schemes; half of all schemes with over 5000 members have at least 40 per cent of the places on trustee boards occupied by member trustees, compared with just over one-tenth of smaller schemes.

Table 4.2: The participation profile of trustee boards (pensions manager survey)*

Member trustees as % of all trustees	Percentage of schemes with member trustees
Under 33%	11
33%	14
34 to 40%	19
41 to 49%	23
50%	28
Over 50%	5
	100

*See the Appendix for the bases for this and subsequent tables.

It must be said at once that 'majority' and 'minority' are not terms which are common in trustee board parlance. Votes are very rarely taken, and there is little of the block tactical manoeuvring which characterises the meetings of many other bodies (with or without democratic representation) in industry and elsewhere. A cynic, in fact, might say that members have been accorded such substantial representation precisely because numbers are irrelevant. The formula of $2x + y$ devised by the Bullock Committee is superfluous in the case of trustee boards because decision-making is by consensus. Disagreement can of course occur, but the dominant mode of decision-making is not that of counting heads.

Yet we need to go further than the simple quantitative degree of member representation. The trend to single coverage schemes makes it quite possible for all employees to be members of the same scheme, so that even the managing director would be technically eligible to serve as a member trustee. In practice the most senior levels of management still usually have their own de luxe schemes, and in any case in the board profiles senior management could not qualify as 'member trustees'. Even so, member trustees are drawn disproportionately from higher occupational levels. Aggregating all trustees together into very crude occupational categories, we get the following picture in boards where there is some member representation: representatives of management occupy exactly 50 per cent of the places and member trustees 45 per cent including pensioners with 2 per cent and full-time union officials with 1 per cent. (The remaining 5 per cent is mainly composed of non-executive directors from outside the company.) Of the member trustees, about two-fifths (16 per cent of the total) were drawn from middle or junior management – twice the level of representation from manual employees, who mustered only about 8 per cent. The remainder were non-managerial white-collar staff.

The occupational composition of member trustees is therefore very uneven. Part of the explanation for this lies in the functional contribution of participation as one part of its rationale: lower managerial levels and other white-collar workers have historically showed a greater concern over pensions, and are presumably better informed about how the system works. They are therefore more likely to present themselves as candidates for selection or appointment to participative bodies, including the board itself. Whether it is justified or not, there is a certain amount of mystique about pensions, and certainly a degree of figurework involved. A correlation between educational levels, confidence in one's own technical ability and occupational position on the one hand, and probability of acting as a member trustee on the other, is therefore not surprising.

This may seem to go slightly against the idea that member trustees should act as a channel of communication between the board and the shop floor, often put forward as a major reason for having member trustees at all. But the board is often only the apex of an elaborate structure of local or regional committees with more broadly based participation. There is, in other words, a hierarchy of representatives which looks reasonably similar to the occupational hierarchy. In this pensions participation resembles other forms of participation, where technical and white-collar staff have often been seen to be most actively involved in company councils and the like.

Representation at trustee level, therefore, is quite widespread and exists in a fair degree of depth, even if its distribution across occupational levels is uneven. The significance of participation as a trend emerges if we turn to look at the *date* at which it was introduced. In the second half of the 1970s, there was a substantial upsurge in the number of trustee boards with some degree of participation. Table 4.3 gives the details.

Table 4.3: Date of introduction of member trustees (pensions manager survey)

Date	Percentage of Schemes with member trustees
Before 1960	17
1961 to 1970	5
1971 to 1975	12
1976 to 1980	52
After 1980	8
No reply	6
	100

Over half the schemes which had some degree of member representation have introduced it within the last ten years, at a time when the general climate was not particularly favourable to the smooth and voluntary extension of participation in other areas. The growth in scheme membership had already taken place by the end of the 1960s, and Table 4.3 shows that this was not accompanied by any noticeable rise in the incidence of participation at that time. The reasons for the emergence of member trustees in significant numbers are dealt with in the next section.

We can now deal with the *methods* by which member trustees are elected or selected. In the pensions manager survey, 14 per cent were simply nominated by management with no prior involvement of scheme members. A further 12 per cent were appointed by management from names put up to them by the membership, so management effectively controlled the selection of at least one-quarter of the member trustees. The largest single category, however, was of direct election by scheme members; 28 per cent of the schemes where participation occurred operated on this basis. In just over a fifth of the schemes, moreover, member trustees were appointed via a joint body such as a consultative committee consisting of management and employee representatives. In 12 per cent of the cases they were selected through trade union channels, and there was a residue of diverse other procedures. Predictably, the member trustee survey provided a rather different picture. Only 3 per cent were selected by management alone, 23 per cent by a joint body and 22 per cent directly through trade union channels. But election by all scheme members was still the most common procedure, with 27 per cent of the total. Both surveys therefore show a higher level of member involvement in the selection process than did the 1978 National Association of Pension Funds survey. Although this reported a level of overall participation similar to the pensions manager survey, almost three-quarters of the member trustees were nominated by management, only 12 per cent by the scheme membership and 2 per cent by trade unions (12 per cent by other methods).

We must look more closely at the notion of representation itself. There is something of an inbuilt contradiction here. For in most bodies in which people act as representatives, they are there (as their name implies) to represent the interests of those who have placed them there, directly or indirectly. Naturally this is not their sole function, and they may on occasion subordinate it to some wider good. MPs, for example, are expected to look after the interests of their constituency, not only in taking up the problems of individual constituents but also in pressing for the area to be fairly treated in the allocation of public resources such as regional grants. Despite this, they may feel obliged to support a general policy which goes against the interests of their own constituents: it would be conceivable, though not probable, that an MP from a mining constituency would favour the promotion of nuclear energy as a source of power even though it might have dire consequences for the future of the coal industry. Representatives are expected to strike some balance between defending the interests of their own constituents and furthering the interests of the population as a whole.

All this takes on a different hue in the case of member trustees. They may be elected on a regional basis, or from a particular plant or section, and the election may be a model of democratic practice. But they are enjoined by law to look after the interests of all the members together, not a particular segment. So the balance between the interests of the constituency and those of the 'electorate' as a whole is irrelevant. Formally, indeed, the 'constituents' should not judge the member trustee at all on the basis of what he or she has done for them, but only on their competence in acting on behalf of all members of the scheme. So one of the pillars of representative democracy – the accountability of the representative to his or her members – is knocked somewhat askew.

As yet this is somewhat theoretical. Where elections to the trustee board take place they are rarely contested, and the record of the trustee is seldom 'on the line' when his period of office is over. But it points to an issue which is often glossed over, but which may well emerge more prominently in the future: the potential divergence of interests between different segments of the membership population. Already this has been exposed in the treatment accorded to early leavers, whose penalisation improves the benefits of stayers, and it could well take on a broader application if the use of the funds becomes a more contested issue and members, better informed than they now are, take different views of the strategy to be pursued. But in any event there is an inherent tension between the natural feeling that a trustee board should be reasonably balanced in its composition, and the legal implication that such a balance is unnecessary and maybe even harmful in suggesting that trustees have specific loyalties within the membership.

Reasons for the Growth in Member Trustees

The reasons for the growth in member representation which occurred in the late 1970s may be summarised under five headings: logic, function, legitimation, law and threat. The *logic* of the case for participation derives from the acknowledgement of pensions as deferred pay, discussed in Chapter 2. The analogy is not strictly accurate, in that the contributions which generate the eventual pension are not available to individuals to dispose of as they see fit; there is no gigantic piggy-bank which employees are able finally to break into the day they retire. The money which has been paid in by the employer and (in the case of a contributory scheme) by the employee stays in the fund, generating the revenue out of which pensions are provided. Where pensions are transferable the sum moves with the employee from one fund to another, but not as if he or she were transferring an account from one bank to another. The money is not alienable. Yet once the principle of deferred pay is acknowledged it drastically undermines the rationale for refusing to allow those to whom the pay is due a say in its management.

There are positions which reject this logic, or at least its apparent implications for participation. It is argued that employers are responsible in the last resort for paying the pension. Once they have undertaken this obligation, it is up to them to discharge the responsibility as they see fit. The 'pay' is not therefore construed as the tangible contribution to the fund, but the promise to pay in the future. The fund does not belong to the employees; only the revenues from it which are adequate to pay their pensions. This was exactly the reasoning behind the Type A management structure outlined at the end of Chapter 2, where pensions were firmly included in the bargaining process but representation equally firmly excluded from the management of the fund. The other line of argument is more paternalist, in varying degrees. It may not dispute the principle of deferred pay, but holds that the management of the scheme is a purely professional business. It would be damaging the employees' own interests to allow them to risk impairing the efficiency of the scheme and leaving themselves with reduced benefits. They therefore have no active part to play in the administration of the scheme or the management of its assets.

An alternative approach to taming the logic of deferred pay differentiates between areas appropriate for employee representation. This may mean allowing participation in consultative committees but not on the trustee board. Or it may mean allowing member trustees but excluding them from decisions on investment matters, which are reserved to company-appointed trustees, usually on the ground that they are professionally equipped to handle financial matters. This is explored in more detail in Chapter 6. The general point here is that in spite of these restrictions the right to participation has been broadly established as a right not a concession, a right moreover that derives from a certain notion of property, however vague.[9]

The *functional* justification for participation has perhaps more force at organisational levels below that of the trustee board. As the schemes have grown, their administration has become more complex. This is partly because of their increased size, but also because the merging of companies has meant that several schemes might have to be brought together into a consolidated whole. Fixed retirement ages have decayed so that there is wider variety of options to be coped with as people choose to retire at very different ages – even if we have only just begun to experience the full force of this trend. Like all social benefits, pensions have become more complicated in responding to rapid changes in economic circumstances and social tastes. To handle this complexity on a professional basis would be an expensive business for many organisations, and the expertise is in any case often hard to come by. By drawing in members of the scheme as representatives on pension committees at a whole number of levels, managements have built themselves a new arm of personnel administration – at relatively little cost, though it would be wrong to suggest that this appeared as a major consideration. Local pension representatives are available to advise individual members on their problems, often building up quite a specialist knowledge of the field.

Trustees do concern themselves with some of the day-to-day aspects of scheme administration, especially where there is no substantial infrastructure of local representation. But the functional rationale for member trustees is primarily of another kind: the transmission of information upwards from the shop floor to assist in policy decisions at board level. The Occupational Pensions Board envisages all trustees as the eyes and ears of the members (OPB, 1982, p. 47). Member trustees in particular are expected to articulate the needs of members and help the board to be more responsive to them. Conversely, they can also transmit information downwards. Cultural and class divisions are revealed by several comments from managerial representatives to the effect that 'they [member trustees] speak the language so they can get the message across'. The degree to which participation is genuinely functional is difficult to assess, since the companies which are most favourable to it are likely to be those who also make most effort to communicate with their members, but it is undoubtedly seen as a positive reason for promoting member representation.

The third reason, closely associated, is *legitimation*. As the schemes grew in membership numbers and asset size, they moved more into the public eye. A range of agents began to develop an interest in them, from the members themselves through analysts concerned with the behaviour of capital to representatives of political parties. The prolonged debate which culminated in the 1975 Social Security Pensions Act meant that at least those interested in pensions policy were posing questions about the management of the schemes. Anyone reading the tea-leaves in the early 1970s could have made a fair guess that pension schemes would not be left quietly alone. Against this background, involving member representatives in their management serves two purposes. To the internal audience, the members, it provides some reassurance that their interests are being safeguarded. Such reassurance is not necessarily very firmly based in actuality, given the limited extent to which member trustees have been able to monitor the performance of the funds, but it exists. Secondly, the presence of member trustees goes some way to legitimating the occupational pension scheme system as a whole in the eyes of the public and of the politicians. It strengthens the argument that a major change in the system would infringe on the rights of future pensioners, for it is obviously more plausible to argue this if members can be shown to be involved in the running of the scheme than if it is all in the hands of the professionals.

Fourthly, a small boost to participation was given by the *law*. The 1975 Act obliged employers to consult with trade unions over whether or not their scheme should be contracted in or out. Law has been largely eschewed by all political parties as a means of promoting participation, and this single instance is not of major significance. Other countries, such as Denmark, Germany, Netherlands, Sweden and even Switzerland, have statutory requirements for participation in the management of their schemes (OPB, 1975). But the 1975 provision helped to strengthen the feeling that pensions is an appropriate area for joint management.

Much more important was the *threat* of legally enforced representation contained in the 1976 White Paper on the role of members in the running of schemes. Its central feature was the proposal that there should be mandatory representation on trustee boards, with equal numbers of management and employee representatives, based on recognised trade unions. This provoked a very hostile response from employers and spokesmen from the pensions industry. Their fire was directed not so much at the idea of parity, but at the proposal that representation should be based on the single channel principle, through trade unions.

The White Paper was directly in line with the policy of the Labour government of the time to strengthen the role of unions as partners in the management of industry (see Chapter 1). The whole thrust of the government's strategy was towards a corporatist approach to industry policy, setting management and unions on as equal a footing as possible, with the state occupying the third corner of the triangle. At national level this was epitomised by an incomes policy which aimed at persuading negotiators to cede some of their traditional bargaining freedoms in support of the struggle against inflation. By the time the White Paper on pensions was published this approach was already coming apart at the seams. The government found it difficult to maintain political momentum and eventually felt obliged to conclude a pact with the Liberals, who were opposed to mandatory forms of participation such as the White Paper put forward. As a result, its proposals never came very close to realisation, but the very fact of their publication prompted pensions managers to think harder about introducing participation.

Whether such moves are termed 'voluntary' is in part a matter of taste, or of philosophical debate. The vast majority of managers rejected the idea that the White Paper was a prime factor in their decisions to introduce participation. Certainly the initiative to introduce member trustees almost invariably came from the management side and not from unions actively drawing on the arguments put forward in the White Paper. But there is little doubt that the prospect of legislation concentrated minds. At a National Association of Pension Funds conference debating whether or not to issue a code on participation, one speaker identified two broad reasons in favour. The first was the straightforward domestic one of giving guidance to NAPF members. The other was '...the political reason. By issuing a voluntary code and encouraging the voluntary spread of participation the Association may preempt legislation; or even if it fails in that objective the guide may at any rate act as a model or point the direction for the legislators. I think this is the primary reason' (Cole, 1981). It is clear that some members had already acted; the point was directed at the laggards. It is also clear, however, that as the threat of legislation receded, so did the impetus behind the voluntary moves towards participation: the debate within the NAPF fizzled out, a 1981 publication from the pensions industry entitled *Pension Fund Trusteeship in the 1980s* gave member trustees only the occasional passing reference and, as Table 4.3 shows, the growth curve flattened out abruptly in the early part of the 1980s.

This chapter has been primarily and rather cursorily descriptive, covering the functions of trustees and the emergence of a substantial degree of participation a trustee level – though I have already qualified that by looking a little more closely at the character of the participants. Chapter 6 presents an assessment of the impact of trustee participation so far, which will give some substance and colour to the necessarily rather legalistic and formal complexion of this chapter. Certainly it is worth stressing here that it is the institutional practice and routines of decision-making that count for as much as the formal structure which participation inhabits – even in a field like pensions, where the legal contours are relatively prominent.

Notes

1. Thus Espinosa and Zimbalist title their book 'Economic Democracy: Workers' Participation in Chilean Industry 1970-73'. They concentrate their analysis on the (favourable) impact of worker participation in terms of economic performance. They open the book with a conceptual discussion on different notions of worker participation and industrial democracy, but do not elaborate on the relation between these and 'economic democracy'. Although the participative firms which they describe in Chile do not take the standard capitalist form but fall within the so-called 'social property' sector involving a measure of public ownership, 'economic' in this approach refers primarily to the effect of participation, not its form.
2. 'Mass distribution of equity stakes in conventional enterprises' is, for Samuel Brittan, 'a probably necessary part of a programme for restoring the price mechanism to its rightful place as the one non-dictatorial method of regulating the economy at high employment' (Brittan 1984, p. 7)
3. The topic was already under discussion in the early 1970s when the Labour Party published an Opposition Green Paper entitled *Capital and Equality* (1973). The inclination there was more towards the proposed Danish system, but was never given substantial impetus.
4. Whilst acknowledging that pension schemes in the UK have a relatively good record of financial stability, the Wilson Committee commented that 'it is unsatisfactory in our view that so much of it [the framework within which the schemes operate] depends on a body of trust law developed for quite other purposes' (1980, p. 324).
5. We have already seen (p. 15) that this was one of the issues which the Wilson Committee described as an area of concern.
6. In 1979 the 90 000 schemes in the private sector covered a total of 6.1 million members; 4.9 million of these were concentrated in under 3000 schemes. Of the total pension assets at the same date, £53 billion, £16 billion were in private schemes invested with insurance companies (GAD, 1981).
7. Results of the 1983 survey have not been published at the time of writing.
8. Some had no trustees, in most cases because the organisation in question was a local authority.
9. This was reflected, indeed, in the Wilson Committee's recommendation (1980) that the practice of equal numbers of member and management representatives on trustee boards should be actively promoted.

5 Controlling Owners

Ownership and Control

Participation is about power and its distribution, about the relationships which exist between individuals and groups of individuals within a framework of institutional practices. Who has what sort of influence over the decision-making process and its outcomes? The question cannot be discussed satisfactorily in the abstract, but must be related to more or less specific areas of decision. Chapter 4 sketched out the functions of trustees: the setting and monitoring of investment policy; the fashioning and application of scheme rules; the supervision of professional managers and advisers; the dissemination of information and the exercise of discretionary powers. The actual impact of participation on these areas is assessed in the next chapter, but the first two, referring to the control of capital, require a more extensive, two-part treatment. There are not only the decisions over how the funds are to be invested but also the use of funds once invested to exercise some measure of control over the recipient, especially where the investment goes into public companies in the form of equity capital.

If you see a new office block going up in the main square of your town, the chances are that it is being built for a pension fund, or several funds. We have already seen in broad terms how pension funds have emerged as major owners of property, as well as of government debt. But for those concerned with the control of industry and the impact of different investment policies on corporate performance it is the presence of pension funds as owners of industrial capital in the form of shareholdings which is of most interest. Not that ownership is the dominant factor that it might seem to be. As will become clear, the analysis of how pension funds are controlled underlines the influence which the lending institutions and managers of capital (primarily banks) have over shareholders, the formal owners of capital.

Discussion of the general influence of pension funds on economic performance at national or corporate level is beyond the scope of this book. I must leave it to others to discuss, for example, the ways in which capital accumulation in this form affects interest rates or whether the whole principle of company-based saving of this type is inefficient.[1] The next chapter analyses the role of trustees in shaping the schemes' policy on investment and other areas. Here I set the backcloth by a brief review of the debate over the relationship between the ownership and control of capital, followed by an account of the network of agents and institutions in which pension funds are embedded.

In so far as 'capitalism' consists largely of privately owned enterprise, the question of control within a capitalist economy has traditionally centred round two interrelated issues: the balance between public (commonly interpreted as state) and private ownership, and the relationship between the owners and the managers of capital. As far as the first of these is concerned, it is obvious that the growth of pension funds has made a simple public/private polarity even more difficult to sustain, even if the implications of this evolution are often not reflected in political analysis or rhetoric. It has also reshaped the distribution of private ownership, although the mere fact that pension fund holdings now outnumber individual holdings of quoted stock cannot be directly converted into an equivalent power shift. It is the relationship between the ownership and management of capital which concerns us here, and the emergence of the funds has contributed to a recasting of the issue into two parts: the longer-standing one of the relationship between the owners of capital and the managers of the *companies* in which the capital is invested, and the newer one of the parallel relationship between the owners and the managers of *financial institutions*. I shall argue that in neither case is it fruitful to frame the issue simply in terms of how far there is a 'divorce' between ownership and management; the task is rather to map out the multiple overlaps and intersections between the agents and institutions involved, in order to achieve a better understanding of the different patterns of control. Only then can the links between capital ownership and corporate behaviour be explored.

The relationship between property and rights has a long history in political theory (Ryan, 1984). With the growth of the joint stock company, ownership by a single person was replaced by multiple ownership as the demand of companies for capital grew beyond the compass of even the most affluent of individuals. It soon became clear that this entailed something other than a broadening of the capitalist class. Marx's analysis of private capital pointed to the tendency for ownership to become progressively concentrated, with strains developing between the private nature of ownership and the increasingly social character of relations at the workplace. But the approach to ownership adopted by some of those who followed Marx was tied to an oversimplified notion of property rights as giving unambiguous control of the means of production.

> If these means are in private hands this gives these private owners control over their use and disposition. If they are in public hands one clear agency of control is displaced by another. This conception of property raises the problems that (a) rights of possession in law are always particular rights, constrained in their exercise by both laws which construct these rights and other laws, and (b) the use of means of production is constrained by a variety of non-legal practices. (Tomlinson, 1982, pp. 18–19)

In other words, the legal title itself does not give unadulterated power to owners, public or private, and the power that it does afford has to be balanced against a variety of other powers, including that of collective labour.

From a very different political perspective to that of Marx, the 1928 Liberal Industrial Inquiry on 'Britain's Industrial Future' promoted the separation of ownership and control as a hopeful sign that socialism was unnecessary:

> The divorce between responsibility and ownership worked out by the growth and development of Joint Stock Companies, an event which has occurred since the dogmatic ideas of Socialists took shape, together with the prominence of legitimate tendencies towards combinations, cartels and Trade Associations, provide one of the clues to the future. Private enterprise has been trying through the past fifty years to solve for itself the essential problem which the Socialists in their day were trying to solve, namely, how to establish an efficient system of production in which management and responsibility are in different hands from those which provide the capital, run the risk and reap the profit. (1928, p. 100)

The solution has proved less easy to find than the Report's sanguine tone suggests. In the following decade the topic was given substantial theoretical attention by the American authors Berle and Means (1932). The 'managerialist' thesis which they put forward argued that there was an increasing dissociation between ownership and control, with managers being left in charge of company policy, taking their decisions largely independently of the (usually unarticulated) wishes of individual shareholders. The thrust of the argument as it developed over subsequent decades was that ownership was becoming less and less relevant as running a company became more and more a matter of technical expertise. A blurring of the descriptive and normative took place as companies grew in size and complexity and the technocratic ideology expanded commensurately. Its message was that the management of major companies is in the hands of salaried professionals, who do not necessarily have a direct financial stake in the enterprise. Shareholders large and small receive dividends and see their capital grow, but are not involved - and do not expect to be involved - in determining corporate growth. It is the managers who decide on the balance between profit maximisation and other forms of corporate growth. They do so in the name of economic efficiency, but also with some regard for other considerations such as stability. Capitalism had been tamed, or emasculated, depending on one's viewpoint.

The thesis flowered in the 1960s. In the US, J.K. Galbraith's notion of a dominant 'technostructure' encouraged the image of management as a professional activity, having - or aspiring to - the sort of autonomy enjoyed by other professionals and claiming as the basis for this autonomy a similar degree of technical expertise. Politically, the managerialist thesis provided the basis for the position whose foremost British exponent was Anthony Crosland. The essence of its case was that ownership, for so long the touchstone of socialist thinking and the key issue on which the political Right and Left were to be distinguished, no longer deserved to occupy a central position in either theoretical analysis or policy formulation. The implication was that political discussion should concentrate directly on the how of control, not the whether of public ownership. The task was to improve corporate efficiency and then to achieve the political goal of a more equitable distribution of the fruits of that efficiency. Remarkably, the notion of 'efficiency' was taken to be largely unproblematic. It is equally remarkable how little progress has been made subsequently in refining and developing it beyond orthodox financial criteria.[2]

The points made above on the ambiguity surrounding the notion of property apply to the debate on the managerialist thesis as much as to some Marxist approaches. There is, for instance, a failure to distinguish 'ownership', a legal category, from 'possession', which has a far broader social connotation.[3] Even in the context of traditional joint stock companies the notion of 'ownership' is not immediately clear, let alone its implications for the control of company policy and practice. It is often left uncertain what is actually at stake in terms of the ability to control specific policy decisions or actual behaviour.

Moreover, the way the opposition is drawn between owners and managers gives the debate a highly personalised flavour, as if conflict consists in disagreements expressed by individuals in the boardroom or on the floor of the Annual General Meeting. There is a tendency to concentrate on the agents involved, implicitly portraying them as informed, purposeful and homogeneous entities. The focus on individual firms and on personal motivations abstracts the practice of ownership and management from its political and economic context and underplays the driving momentum of the capitalist system. The critics of managerialism themselves rarely spell out either how far they are defining 'capitalism' directly in terms of ownership or precisely how the specifically capitalist features of the system impinge upon the agents, but they are right to remind us of the limits on individual autonomy. On the other hand to treat the individuals involved simply as 'the personification of social relationships' (De Vroey, 1975) is to ignore serious questions about the importance of human agency, as Giddens has pointed out:

> Institutions do not just work 'behind the backs' of the social actors who produce and reproduce them...If actors are regarded as cultural dopes or mere 'bearers of a mode of production', with no worthwhile understanding of their surroundings or the circumstances of their action, the way is immediately laid open for the supposition that their views can be disregarded in any practical programmes that might be inaugurated. (1979, pp. 71-2)

Both these issues – the notion of 'ownership' and the relationship between agency and structure – apply to the control exercised by pension funds over companies, the control of the funds themselves and the role of member trustees.

One approach to the control of individual units of capital is to deny outright the relevance of the shifts which have taken place in the pattern of ownership. At its crudest, this takes the form of arguing that under capitalism market forces are such as to force company management into profit-maximising behaviour, irrespective of the distribution of shareholdings (Blackburn, 1972). Not only is this open to exactly the point made by Giddens above; it also depends on a literally meaningless – because all-embracing – notion of profit maximisation. The behaviour of a profit-maximiser who operates with a time perspective of a few months will be quite different from that of someone who looks to maximise profits over a ten-year period. The very meaning of the term is contingent on the timescale adopted, and to lump all the different possible strategies together is to empty the motive of any significance. This type of argument ignores, moreover, variations in the values held by different agents, in market circumstances, and in the strength of organised labour. A more sophisticated variant holds that owners and managers may now be more distinguishable as groups but the distinction has little significance for the control of capital since the two groups share a common ideology. Even though managers may not have major shareholdings in the companies in which they are employed, their values and behaviour will not differ significantly from those who own the shares. Nichols (1969) is one author who has given this argument an empirical base but an admittedly small one, his study being of 15 firms in the North of England. It puts great weight on the elusive concept of ideology; written before the major expansion of institutional shareholdings it does not deal with the complexity and variety of ownership patterns.

In the 1970s, the focus shifted to a closer scrutiny of the distribution of shareholdings. Ownership was acknowledged as more dispersed, but it was argued that the very fact of its dispersion allowed minority ownership to carry with it a substantial measure of control. Analysis concentrated heavily on size of shareholding even where it was recognised that it is not the only criterion for control. Estimates for the proportion needed to cross the threshold of control varied widely, and an extensive review of American and British studies on the separation of ownership and control concluded that 'because the results are highly sensitive to the methods of firm classification – and the methods do vary considerably from study to study – the research has produced little agreement on the proportion of firms now in the hands of management' (Useem, 1984, p. 29).

In the 1930s Berle and Means had taken the view that unless at least 20 per cent of the stock was concentrated in a single owner the corporation was essentially in the control of the managers. More recent surveys put the threshold of control far lower, going down as far as 4 per cent, and the analysis usually includes some elements other than the crude distribution of shareholdings. To take just one example: Nyman and Silberston focussed their study on the percentage of votes owned by the board and their families, but added in the identity and contact network of the Chairman and Managing Director as significant factors. They assumed 'potential control...to be present with a shareholding of more than 5%' (1978, p. 84).

Reviewing the various approaches, Cubbin and Leech (1983) point out that the choice of size of shareholding is generally arbitrary, and the measure of control is usually reduced to a simple opposition between ownership-control and management-control. They themselves suggest instead an approach which views the question of control in terms of 'degree' and 'location' with a number of positions being possible on each of these dimensions.[4] Subsequent refinements will surely pull the issue further away from a simple dichotomy, but the more recent studies contain a further shift in the focus of analysis. They introduce financial institutions as major agents in the pattern of control. Banks in particular, but also insurance companies and pension funds, are included alongside individual shareholders as significant influences on the distribution and use of capital. The more they are seen as important, the more the question of control is pushed back to include the control of the institutions themselves as well as the control of industrial enterprises.[5]

On the broad plane of political economy, the growth of financial institutions forms part of the debate over the relationship between financial and industrial activity. Conceptually, it has involved intricate distinctions between different types of capital – banking, finance, industrial, entrepreneurial and monopoly – and the variety of possible relationships and hierarchies between them. Broadly speaking, there are two main lines of argument over whether one type of capital predominates over the others. The first is that in the UK at least there has been a progressive subordination of industrial to finance capital. Rubinstein (1977) presents a historical account which suggests that there was a prolonged rivalry between the two, with an added geographical dimension to the tension. The outcome, in the 1930s, was subordination of Northern industrial capital to Southern and metropolitan finance capital. The City financier, following Jim Slater's advice and making money out of money, triumphed over the archetypal Yorkshire businessman who made brass out of muck. Internationally, the UK is contrasted with countries such as West Germany and Japan where the relationship between finance and industry is closer and more balanced (Longstreth, 1979; Prais, 1982).

An alternative line of argument suggests that it is wrong to see the two sectors as in clearcut opposition to each other. Parasitic or not, the financial sector needs industry for its own success, so that there is a complex, if often unstable, pattern of interdependence between the two. Scott observes that 'the development from personal to impersonal possession is associated with an integration and interdependence between the financial and industrial sectors of the economy' (1979, p. 94) but refers to the different forms this interdependence has historically taken in different countries. The position is complicated by the exceptionally international orientation of the British financial sector, an overstrained valve in the pulsating heart of the world capital market, and by the fact that many of its activities are fundamentally commercial in character. They thus involve the selling of financial services on a day-to-day basis rather than the assertion of continuing financial control via capital holdings (Ingham, 1984).

Institutional Control

The nature of the relationship between ownership and control depends in part on the level of detail at which the analysis is pitched (as well as on the timespan adopted). Our present concern is at the level of individual companies, and the role played by pension funds as one part of the financial sector. What is it that is being controlled? Broadly speaking the control of public companies embraces both the supply of funds (including the threat of their withdrawal) and the management of the company (including the composition of its board of directors).[6] But it should be stressed that in either case control need not be exercised overtly. As Coakley and Harris observe in pointing out the apparent low level of institutional influence:

> We would not expect to find evidence of much implicit intervention in companies' financial decisions, for intervention would occur only if control were slipping. The most effective influence occurs through companies knowing they always have to satisfy these investors and thus formulate their policies appropriately to ensure that the watching sleeper stays asleep. (1983, p. 115)

Some examples of explicit intervention are given later. But here we are concerned with more general patterns of influence.

Some empirical evidence on the extent to which control has passed from individual owners to financial institutions comes from the Oxford study of large firms. Francis (1980) suggests that the distribution of a firm's shareholdings is only a first approximation as a measure of power and that a better second approximation involves examining who the chairman is and how he came to be appointed. This in turn entails matching changes in company behaviour and performance with changes in the composition of the board, as the board may or may not be in tune with the chairman. A survey of over 200 top firms in the UK and longitudinal analysis of changes in a sub-sample show that ownership is still a powerful factor, understated by simple shareholding figures; but also that financial institutions, especially banks, are assuming an increasing share of control. There are a number of caveats to the argument. In parallel to the argument that the division between owner-control and management-control is not a straightforward dichotomy, the roles of financial and industrial capital in controlling British companies should not be approached dichotomously. This is a plurality of interests at work, and no exclusive form of control. Francis also warns that it is misleading to lump all financial institutions together as if they exhibited the same behaviour and values. (For example, one needs to distinguish between those whose main investment interest is in equities and those who deal mainly in loan stock.) The focus of their activities will naturally shape the vigour and direction of their attempts to control capital. Finally, there is as yet little evidence on the impact of different types of control on company behaviour.

The Oxford study does not deal specifically with pension funds, but in combination these caveats suggest that overall conclusions about the influence of financial institutions are possible only at a very generalised level. This reservation may be extended further. One might be able to make certain distinctions between broad categories of financial institution (say pension funds and insurance companies) in their impact on industry – there is evidence, for example, that pension funds deal marginally less actively in the stock market. But within these broad categories further sub-division is not only possible but fruitful for a different level of understanding. Thus local authority and other public-sector funds deal less actively than private-sector funds, but these formal categories are not the only ones possible: one could divide the funds according to the industrial sector within which the company concerned is located or by the size of total assets, and so on. We are a long way from being clear about which of these dimensions are particularly significant, and in what respects. They are, moreover, cross-cut both by the personal characteristics of individual agents and by routine practices which exist within every institution but to different degrees.

This does not mean that we must wait for perfect information to be available before any conclusions can be drawn. It does suggest that simply to identify different institutions, or sets of institutions, as potentially controlling agents may be to replicate to a degree the weakness of classifying shareholders according to the proportions of shares they hold and proceeding to assess their power accordingly. Different forms of property yield different sets of rights, and these not only change over time themselves but are constrained by changing sets of economic and social circumstances. Even when the single dichotomy between public and private ownership was broadly valid its implications for the distribution of power could not be read off like a logarithm table. The significance of institutional ownership, especially where the institutions are themselves of uncertain proprietorial character, is hard to assess without more direct information about their composition and modes of operation.

Figure 5.1 brings us down from the abstractions which have been so far presented, perhaps rather indigestibly, to a simple descriptive level. It sets out – admittedly in incomplete form – the lines of influence which run to and from pension funds in their position as owners of equity capital. Such a scheme runs inevitable risks. The lines distinguish between ownership and influence but do not allow for different forms of ownership – for example individual pension scheme members do not have the same ownership rights as individual shareholders. Moreover, the image of the arrow suggests a direct and clean line of influence; the reality is almost always fuzzier, cocooned in a mass of formal and informal practices and codes. But it should help to show how a particular type of institution – or rather, particular instances of a type – fits into a certain network, where the routines of financial decision-making tie individuals and corporate bodies into a series of more or less close and collective embraces.

Even in schematic form it is impossible to trace out all the relevant

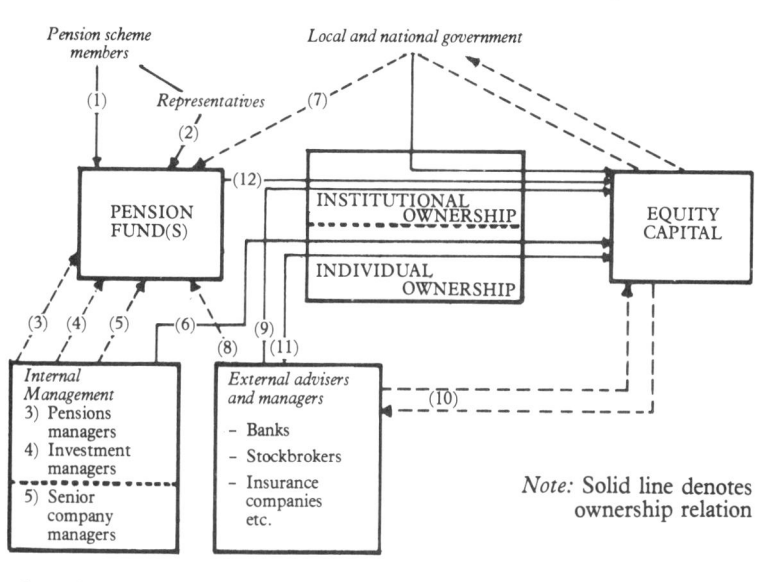

Figure 5.1: Lines of influence running to and from pension funds in their position as owners of equity capital.

lines of influence without engaging in an exercise of Heath Robinsonian draughtsmanship. I have left out, for example, solid lines running from managers to pension funds (as pension scheme members), and from non-managerial individual pension scheme members to companies (as individual shareholders). More significantly, insurance companies are not included as a separate category, though they have a substantial stake in managing smaller funds and stand to increase their role enormously if the present proposals for personal pensions go through. To repeat, the purpose is modest: to provide a simplified means of grasping something of the range of relationships surrounding the central relationship between pension funds and industrial capital.

One further caveat. The diagram and the accompanying discussion are by way of backcloth to the analysis of member trusteeship and its impact. The lines are far from being all of the same thickness, as it were. There is a natural temptation to bolster the significance of one's subject. In the case of pension fund trustees there is an understandable interest – almost titillation – in the idea that 'ordinary' members of the workforce should be in a position to make decisions on the fate of millions of pounds. There is also often the political ambition that this might be so, as a more accountable and democratic form of decision-making. But line 2 is not the dominant line. Compared with the direct influence of bankers and with the ingrained force of financial practices, the activities of trustees are very probably influential only to a minimal degree. 'Probably', because we await a balanced and comprehensive treatment of the network as a whole. This book traces in detail only one strand of the web that I shall now describe.

Line 1 refers to the possibility that individual pension scheme members might exert control over the fund directly. It is open to them to express their views to the company or to the trustees on any issue. In the nature of things this is likely to be on a matter which affects the member personally, such as the criteria used for making discretionary decisions. But a member could in principle attempt to influence the fund's investment policy, criticising its performance or suggesting a particular line of action with regard to a particular investment. The chances of this occurring to any significant degree are rather less than those of a shareholder influencing a major company by brandishing a single share certificate at the Annual General Meeting.

Where they have representation (line 2), the chances of members exercising a degree of control are higher. This is the subject of the next chapter, so there is no need to explore it in detail here. It is worth simply repeating that although it is only through member trustees that there is member involvement in fund policy, the conduct and outcome of collective bargaining may be highly relevant. Negotiations do not cover investment strategy, let alone the policy of the fund towards individual companies, but the line between negotiation over benefits and participation in trusteeship is not as watertight as is sometimes suggested.[7]

Lines 3, 4 and 5 refer to management staff on the payroll of the company or of the scheme. (Practice on the division of management costs between company and scheme is diverse and often blurred. For example, staff salaries and computer costs may be assumed by the company as part of its own overheads.) The need for separate lines illustrates how important it is to be clear at what level of generality one is operating in discussing management and control. The positing of a division between 'owners' and 'managers' suggests two homogeneous classes who may or may not share the same values. We have already noted (p. 44) that pensions managers and other managers may well diverge in their attitude to the value of pensions. But even the class of people officially designated as 'pensions managers' covers a diverse group of employees. Schematically, two opposing types can be discerned. The first is the 'pensioneer'. He has been concerned with pensions all or most of his professional life and his chief concern is with the welfare side. He became involved in pensions management when the scheme's assets were relatively insignificant and pensions a genuinely fringe benefit. He may be faintly bemused to find himself involved in decisions of major import to the organisation's balance sheet. On the other side is the 'financier'. A more recent phenomenon, he has emerged to take over responsibility for pensions as a consequence of dawning corporate awareness of their financial significance. He is probably professionally qualified in accountancy or some other field of financial expertise. The post of pensions manager is a stepping stone in the path to a senior executive position. With little interest in the welfare side (though perhaps some in industrial relations) his prime goal is to keep tight control over pension costs.

The varying backgrounds, skills and values of pensions managers necessarily affect their attitudes to trustees (and member trustees), to financial advisers and to the membership. Certainly such factors affect the extent to which they seek to influence investment policy (line 3). A 'pensioneer' is more likely to rely totally on external advice, and expect his trustees to do likewise. The prime example of this type from the Glasgow case studies would not dream of intervening in the detail of investment strategy. Indefatigable in touring the company's consultative committees and wholeheartedly committed to the welfare of the scheme members, he would barely regard the Stock Exchange as worth an afternoon's visit. The financier, on the other hand, will actively collaborate with professional advisers, to ensure that the fund performs well and minimises the company's burden of contributions. Just as full-time managers in ordinary companies are strongly placed to influence policy compared with part-time or outside directors and with shareholders, so even a welfare-oriented pensions manager's day-to-day involvement gives him a potentially significant influence on investment policy.

This simple typology obviously provides a very limited insight into pensions managers. Certainly some will be members of the small class of individuals who hold shares themselves, as will their fellow-managers (line 6). The point is not that they might be influenced by holding shares in the same companies as their employing scheme's fund, but that their ideology may be assumed to be that of the orthodox capitalist, however that is construed. Fancifully one might suppose that pensions managers compensate for the sober responsibilities of their occupational role by acting the dashing entrepreneur with their own funds. In practice, continuity of behaviour is more likely than compensation.

In some schemes an investment manager – or even several – is employed as a member of staff (line 4). This is where the size of the fund is sufficient to justify a salary and attendant costs, instead of fees paid to external agents. Clearly an investment manager has a major influence, perhaps even the dominant one. He, after all, not only handles the money but is responsible for the bulk of the information distributed on investment to the trustees, and onwards to the members. But an investment manager rarely if ever acts entirely on his own, and his influence must be set against that of the external advisers which even the biggest funds use. He may well have begun his career as a stockbroker or merchant banker, and intend to return to that path later on. He may believe – and be attracted by the possibility – that he can in some way do better serving a single fund than a plethora of clients, but the degree of shared values and practice with his financial colleagues is very high. As a full-time investment specialist, his influence is likely to be high, at least in comparison with his internal pensions management colleagues. He will not be so inhibited as the pensioneer is by welfare considerations, nor even by a more general obligation to take industrial relations into account as the financier sometimes is.

We should not leave the category of 'company manager' without mentioning the influence of senior executives who have no formal role within the pension scheme (line 5). The whole rationale for pension schemes is that they are independent of the company, so that pension rights are to some extent secured independently of the fortunes – or eventual misfortune – of the enterprise. This does not stop senior executives taking an active interest in the fund's performance, and in the activities of the trustee board. They have the power to appoint trustees, perhaps even all of them.[8] They may even intimate their wishes overtly. But the power will more often be exercised in a covert way, pre-empting decisions which might depart from their own views of what should be done financially. We should remember that unlike many other areas pensions is a corporate issue where decisions are taken centrally, and this increases the chances that top management will at least look on it as something that is on their level of operation. Pilch and Wood observe that:

> ...it is probably true that significant decisions affecting pension fund finances have been taken with very few exceptions in company board rooms rather than elsewhere. The centre of influence may well shift in future towards collective bargaining between management and unions or employee representatives, and management committees may have a role to play in bringing them together. There appears to be no part that can or should be taken in this process by trustees. (1979, p. 190)

The observation is correct in so far as it refers only to benefit and contribution levels. But the comment that decisions affecting fund finances are taken in company board rooms has a broader application, as senior management appreciates the importance of the fund's management to the corporate financial position. Pension funds can constitute a substantial hidden asset or liability – more probably the former, given their recent net growth. This may, for example, influence the vulnerability of the company to take-over, though the Superannuation Funds Office's rules make straightforward asset-stripping difficult. It certainly means that the management of the fund can be identified as a direct management function, reducing trustees to a marginal role.[9]

The state at national or local level has considerable leverage on the activities of funds and their relationship to industrial capital (line 7). At the most general level, it may do this through broad policy instruments such as the setting of interest rates, attracting funds away from direct investment in industry and into government bonds. The lifting of exchange controls has been a powerful influence on the pattern of pension fund investment behaviour. An alternative political proposal, from the Labour Party, is to discourage the funds from investing abroad by giving fiscal privileges only to those who do not invest more than a certain percentage of their assets abroad. Legal requirements are set by government, for example the conditions of solvency which a scheme must satisfy before it qualifies for its certificate from the Occupational Pensions Board. More specific regulations include the vetting of levels of self-investment, currently set at 10 per cent. And in so far as the judiciary is instrumental in interpreting and implementing state laws, the behaviour of judges in their interpretation of trust law is an increasingly significant factor in defining the contours of the funds' investment behaviour.

The state is of course not homogeneous. In particular we have seen over recent years major strains developing between the central administration and local authorities. Various efforts have been made by some metropolitan authorities to mobilise pension fund money for industrial use; here it is sufficient to note that the local state can seek actively to influence its own superannuation fund and to attract investment from outside funds. At the ideological level, moreover, it is arguable that the initiatives taken – rhetorically or in practice – by Local Enterprise Boards have done something to change the climate in which pension funds' investment policies are fashioned. In particular, the idea that funds should seek to influence the industrial relations and other policies of the companies in which they invest has been most actively promoted at this level.

I have left to the end of the list of influences on the funds the box labelled 'external advisers and managers' (line 8) because it is both complex and carries great weight, and therefore requires rather more elaboration than the rest. Its principal constituent agents are insurance companies, merchant banks, stockbrokers and advisers who deal in a single specialised sector such as property consultants. I shall not attempt to give a full account of the role of each of these, but refer only to their different forms of involvement in the decision-making process.[10]

As the label suggests, they play both an advisory and a management role. At one end of the spectrum is the fully insured fund, where the scheme simply hands over its contributions to an insurance company in return for a guaranteed level of payments. This is particularly the case with the smallest schemes, who are purchasing a financial service with the least frills. Other schemes place all their assets with an insurance company but retain a degree of identity by having them in a 'managed fund', where the returns are more directly related to the performance of the assets. The assets may be specifically assigned to an equity or a property fund, or form part of a mixed fund. Obviously it is the insurance company that does all the actual managing.

The bigger the fund, the more likely it is that there will be a degree of internal management, of the sort I have already outlined. In such cases merchant banks and stockbrokers may be hired as 'advisers', in the sense that they do not actually handle the assets on a day-to-day basis but provide information and technical expertise. In practice the dividing line between the act of management and the provision of advice is predictably thin, especially where the advice is followed more or less implicitly. There is nevertheless an important difference in principle between handing over the fund, or part of it, to a bank and concentrating purely on monitoring the rate of return to the assets, and on the other hand laying down with some degree of specificity a strategy which is to be followed and to which appropriate advice should be geared.

There are differences in the approaches to investment management exhibited by banks and brokers, but these need not concern us here (see Minns, 1980, p. 30 for detail). A fund may employ a single bank as a manager or adviser, or if it is big enough it may choose to employ several, perhaps in the hope of promoting a spirit of productive competition. In one case study the fund used six banks and had taken to systematically dropping one every year or so, presumably 'pour encourager les autres'. This is in a sense a demonstration of power over the adviser by the fund, but its effect on the actual disposition of the assets is less clear. For such an approach may simply shift the external agents' investment strategies to a shorter-term focus so that they can justify themselves on the basis of the annual performance. Yet a short-term focus is regularly deplored both by the orthodox management texts and by more radical critics of current practice.

Trustees are now taking a livelier interest in the performance of their advisers. It remains the case that although a number of external fund managers consistently produce the best results, poor performers still retain a great deal of money to look after. Amongst the reasons given for this are the laxness of some funds in never checking the manager's record against the competition; the forceful marketing techniques adopted by the sellers of financial services; and the fact that advice from pensions consultants is not always unbiased.[11]

The relationship between internal management and external advisers thus runs the gamut between total dependence (as far as investment decisions are concerned) to a position of near-equivalence. Where the internal management role is essentially a welfare or administrative one, the position of the manager is roughly that of a consumer purchasing a technical service of which he understands little and often at a price which is far from clearly defined. In the pensions manager survey, less than a quarter reported some sort of system for monitoring investment costs, although there is growing sophistication in the techniques used for performance measurement.

The manager may still be able to exercise consumer choice (through the trustees), though the variety between banks and therefore the extent to which he is able to shop around is still limited. He may even be able to exert some consumer power in negotiating fees or querying charges. But the discussion on financial policy will not be on a remotely equal basis. Where, on the other hand, there is internal management which is strong on financial expertise, their relationship with the advisers will be essentially collegial, tapping into the banks' greater resources from a position of rough professional parity.

The latter end of the spectrum is, however, a rarity. Minns summarises the picture as follows:

> At a certain stage in the development of a pension fund the trustees, or directors or (in the case of local authorities) panel, may decide to manage the fund 'in house' by employing their own investment manager and investment department. Funds in all three groups of private sector, local authority and other public sectors have decided to do this for all or part of their funds, and with varying degrees of sophistication. Some funds have their own analysts and dealers as well as an investment manager, others have a manager who is dependent upon the information provided by a wide range of stockbrokers but who decides which information to use. Some of these funds are disdainfully described by external managing institutions as 'broker fodder'. (1980, p. 32)

The power of the external advisers does not derive only from the particular expertise they offer to a given fund. Far more significant is the fact that they act on behalf of many funds at the same time. In 1984 the total assets of all pension funds amounted to something over £120 billion. Table 5.1 shows that the top 15 fund managers were responsible between them for well over one-third of this total, each of them handling over £1 billion. The table shows the growth in the assets handled and in the number of clients each has.

These managers – and especially the merchant banks – generally take a

Table 5.1: Leading fund managers, 1984

Manager	Value of funds (£m) 1984	1983	% increase	Number of clients 1984	1983
Warburg	6600	4850	36.1	254	184
Schroders	5750	4500	27.8	131	123
Robert Fleming	4125	3300	25.0	104	102
Phillips & Drew	4000	3100	29.0	134	127
County Bank	3536	2687	31.6	117	78
Barclays Bank	3300	2500	32.0	58	52
Morgan Grenfell	3300	2965	11.3	140	90
Hill Samuel	3100	2700	14.8	175	180
Lloyds Bank	2530	2328	8.7	31	36
N.M. Rothschild	2032	1512	34.4	72	65
Baring Bros	1965	1500	31.0	66	64
Midland Bank	1818	1291	40.8	30	18
Lazards	1600	1250	28.0	52	51
Grieveson Grant	1424	1230	15.7	74	68
Geoffrey Morley	1170	1248	–6.3	41	48

Source: *Financial Times*, 20 February 1985

'top-down' approach to managing their clients' funds. In the case of the biggest – Warburg's – with over 200 clients and almost £7 billion in its portfolio – a five-man investment policy committee meets at least monthly to decide on how the assets are to be allocated. These decisions are then implemented by the bank's 40 fund managers. None of these second-tier managers has more than 12 clients, but it is clear that the decisions of the five members of the chief committee set the course for a vast bulk of investments. Although individual sets of trustees may lay down guidelines – and they are reported now to be intervening more in the fixing of asset allocation – there is no doubting where the overall pattern is determined (Batchelor, 1984).

There is some evidence that the internal control of companies is influenced by interlocking directorates, with individuals sitting on the boards of several companies simultaneously.[12] But this practice pales into insignificance compared with the multiple adviserships of the financial institutions, with banks and brokers acting simultaneously for a whole range of funds. Furthermore, in the very nature of things they can hardly act in isolation from each other, given the geography of the City. What might be called the general investment tone is therefore set to a large extent by a small number of external institutions, cheek by jowl in Lombard Street.

The interweaving of financial institutions is tighter even than this suggests. For the banks act as advisers, and suppliers of capital, to individual companies as well as to pension funds (lines 9 and 10). (Bankers and stockbrokers are of course the most likely people of all to hold shares as individuals – line 11). The link may be a direct one, or via investment trusts in which both the banks and the funds have holdings. A bank may be advising a company going through a sticky period and liable to be fatally crippled if its shareholders lose confidence, and at the same time managing a fund with substantial holdings in that company whose value will drop sharply if the company does indeed fold.[13] At what moment is it right for the bank to wear which hat? Usually these strains are carefully concealed, but they do emerge. Under the headline 'Naughty Warburg', for example, the City correspondent of the *Observer* noted that the City's leading merchant bank:

> ... seems hell-bent on stirring up a meeting between the merchant banks and the pension funds whose investments they manage. On no fewer than four occasions this year (1983), Warburg's actions have exposed dangerous potential conflicts of interest between a bank's corporate advisory division and its investment management department. (*Observer*, 18 December 1983)

The report went on to note that Warburg was advising the House of Fraser board in its highly public and long-running battle to fight off the takeover by Lonrho: at the same time it was managing key stakes held in the House of Fraser company by a number of pension funds.

Now that the 'City revolution' is underway, mergers and takeovers between financial institutions are proceeding apace, so the overall degree of integration will become still closer. Between 1982 and 1984 more than 40 such mergers, or link-up agreements, have been concluded, involving all seven of the top merchant banks and all the five biggest jobbing firms. A prominent example is the emergence of the Mercury International Group (MIG), a £350 million conglomerate assembled by the merchant bank Warburg's and three Stock Exchange firms. The move gives several extra twists to the spiralling complexity of capital management. It

> will produce an intricate web of conflicting interest in the group, between, for example, the investment managers (who will command more than £7.5 billion in client's money), the brokers and market makers and the corporate finance people. Three groups are being created: merchant banking, securities and asset management. The traditional Chinese walls will be erected to prevent information

seeping from one to another and these will be patrolled by full-time 'compliance officers' and equipped with coded locks and limited access lifts. The securities group will also be in a separate building. Employees will be instructed to make clear to clients in what capacity they are acting. (Lascelles, 1985)

Quite how long it will take for employees 'to make it clear to clients' is uncertain; will, for example, their explanation include an explanation of the MIG structure and its multiple commitments? If so, the briefing is likely to be a long one.[14] Where the management of so many funds is concentrated in so few hands, direct conflicts of interest are bound to occur, and potential conflicts lurk under the surface in far greater numbers (Plender, 1982).

Table 5.2: *Ownership and control of listed UK equities, 1980*

	Ownership (%)	Control (%)
Banks	2	22
Insurance companies	19	20
Pension funds	27	9
Trusts	8	5
	56	56

Source: Coakley and Harris, 1983, p. 111

The internal intricacies of banks, their offshoots and their new partners are far too baroque to be included in the compass of our simple diagram. Basing themselves on Minns' analysis, Coakley and Harris constructed a table showing the reallocation between categories of owner when control over equity capital was treated as not determined by ownership alone (see Table 5.2). By far the biggest adjustment is the reduction in the role of pension funds and the converse increase in that of the banks. The Glasgow research also revealed the importance of the banks as external advisers: a bank was identified as the most important external adviser by three times as many pensions managers as any other category of adviser. Our previous discussion indicates that the figures in the table should be treated with caution, to be taken as indicating the parameters of the issue rather than as precise measures; they represent nevertheless a significant realignment of control even before the City revolution got underway. They drive another nail into the coffin of Drucker's thesis that socialism has arrived by the back door, and underline the need to avoid treating institutions as independent agents isolated from the network within which they operate.

Finally, what about line 12, which goes directly from the fund to the firm? The forms of direct or indirect influence which a fund may exercise on firms through its ownership of equity capital can be treated at two levels: influence on policy in companies in which it already has holdings, and the adoption of particular criteria for choosing companies in which to invest. The former refers to the control of capital once it is invested (including its withdrawal); the latter to control over the supply of capital in the first place (including withholding it from particular companies or regions).

1. Shareholder power
In one sense, of course, influence is exercised hourly through the routine trading of shares. Selling shares in a company is an indication, however mild, that the company is not considered to be the best outlet for that part of one's capital. But we are concerned with more explicit forms of influence:

a) *Active shareholdership.* Particular ways in which a firm intends to distribute surplus can be influenced by the fund as a shareholder. Two of the most prominent examples of this in recent years illustrate in raw form the way in which capital holders can refuse to allow corporate management to benefit at their expense. One concerned the proposal by Associated Communications Corporation to make a record compensation payout of £560 000 to its former Managing Director, Jack Gill. The Post Office Staff Superannuation Fund led the successful challenge and the payout was blocked. The same fund led the attack in the second example. It owns about 1 per cent of the equity of Marks and Spencers, whose directors were occupying housing provided by the company at rents very much below their market value – a total of £17 500 compared with about £100 000. In this case the company was obliged under pressure to present the facts to a shareholders' meeting. The amounts are trifling in relation to the company's turnover and to the fund's assets, but the point was made.

As shareholders, the funds can make their views known on the adequacy of corporate management and structure. This may mean sharpening up managerial performance, promoting restructurings or defending against predatory raids companies which are doing well and do not wish to be taken over. At present the funds rarely intervene along these lines, and this passivity has drawn criticism from those who believe that major investors should take a more positive role in monitoring company performance.[15] But there are a growing number of examples of positive intervention, such as the wholesale shake-up of senior management forced upon Rank Organisation in 1983 by a number of institutions including the British Rail and National Coal Board funds. According to the chief investment managers of the Prudential

Assurance, the trend is for greater activity by institutional investors:

> Investment managers cannot properly be expected to challenge managers' business judgements, but they can and should challenge the continuation unchanged of managements with a long record of poor judgement...Gradually pension funds willing and able to act in this way are emerging, most notably from amongst the public sector funds...Such activity seems likely to become more common in future. (Artus and Minto, 1984, p. 39)[16]

These types of action could be termed conventionally capitalist in that they pursue direct financial return. They do not address themselves to questions of broader social responsibilities. Although they may have some moral overtones, the proclaimed rationale is the defence of the shareholders' particular interests, for instance in not having their money spent on unnecessarily generous emoluments. There is a different and rarer category of actions which depart from this rationale (without this entailing that the shareholders' interests are not safeguarded). They proclaim an ethical or social rationale for shareholder action, whether or not this conflicts with the economic rationale. Typically, the fund may try to get the firm to improve its industrial relations practice or its policy on racial or sexual discrimination. It may as a shareholder press for higher standards on pollution control and the working environment. Or it may attempt to achieve a restructuring of the company towards different goals. For example, instead of selling its shares in tobacco companies, the fund may use its voting muscle to get the company to embark on a programme of diversification, so that eventually it may abandon tobacco production altogether without the traumatic employment consequences of an immediate wholesale shift. Another objective might be to get the company to close down its operations in South Africa.[17] If it is not successful, the fund may use its influence in another way – by disinvesting.

b). *Disinvestment.* 1(a) – active shareholdership – refers to the exercise by the funds of their 'voice' (in Hirschman's terminology, see note 6 at the end of chapter), to a number of different tunes. Disinvestment is the institutional version of 'exit': the withdrawal of capital as a protest against the company's performance. Again the protest can be made on purely economic terms – in which case it is simply conventional stock market activity, where shareholders judge that they can get a better return elsewhere on their capital. But it can also be made explicitly on other criteria. I include under this heading the threat of disinvestment, even where the threat is not actually carried through.

The 'clean portfolio' strategy (Baldwin, 1980) is one whose goal is that the fund should not have investments in any company or country which is considered morally unacceptable; existing investments in such areas should be sold off, immediately or in a phased policy. The example most often cited is South Africa, but it is not alone – Chile being a prominent candidate in the 1970s (Purcell, 1979). At enterprise level, anti-smoking movements are seeking to persuade funds to sell their holdings in tobacco companies; or trade unions may try to make sure that the funds in which they have a say withdraw money in firms which exhibit anti-union behaviour. So the same set of objectives may obtain as for active shareholdership.

These are types of disinvestment which are designed to exercise influence directly on the companies concerned – usually explicitly so, unlike the conventional selling of shares. Pension funds can also use the weapon of disinvestment indirectly, to influence company behaviour in one or more of the directions mentioned above. They may do so by threatening exit from the financial institutions which earn large revenues from managing them, pressuring those institutions to disengage from the selected targets – in other words, a kind of double disinvestment process. One of the most celebrated cases of such a tactic was the campaign waged by American unions against the textile firm J.P. Stevens. Mainly by threatening to withdraw their pension funds from the banks handling them, the unions were able to force the institutions to sever their ties with the company. The pressure this generated culminated in union recognition by the company as the price for maintaining its place in the financial community (Barber, 1982). The case illustrates again the nexus which binds together funds, corporations and banks.

2. Alternative investment strategies
In addition to their influence as shareholders in particular companies, pension funds may individually or collectively adopt strategies which influence both the geographical distribution of capital and the types of organisation which have access to their capital. This takes the active shareholdership and disinvestment approaches back a stage and raises them above the microeconomic level. It takes them back a stage in the sense that the decisions on how the capital is to be used are made before the investments take place as distinct from when they are already made; and it raises the level in the sense that the goal is often to influence a particular geographical region or industrial sector rather than an individual company.

This was the line of argument adopted by Rifkin and Barber in *The North Will Rise Again*: their goal was to stem the drain of pension fund capital from the industrial north-eastern states to the non-unionised, regulation-free southern belt. The rationale was in part that the workers to whom the funds belong should not see their jobs and communities undermined by the transfer of the capital to other areas where the immediate economic returns are higher. This kind of approach is now being promoted in a number of states where there is concern about the mobility and accountability of pension fund capital. A review of 'alternative' investment policies cited a number of public employee pension funds which have, in varying degrees, concentrated their investments in their own state or country (Mares, 1979). The aim is to encourage local economic growth, through loans to local businesses, the provision of finance for home loans and the establishment of pooled local investment sources.

These approaches are part of a broader movement towards 'socially responsible' investment, whose goals are to increase local employment by revitalising the economy, to advance social purposes such as low-cost housing and health centres for workers, to improve employees' rights at work and to exclude from investment portfolios companies which are hostile to those rights or transgress in other ways. The central American union federation, the AFL-CIO, has put forward a programme geared specifically to help their pension fund trustees support such aims. It includes the establishment of a co-ordinated information system to give advice on which companies should be regarded as unworthy of investment, and the development of special training for those involved in investment policy.[18]

It is not a coincidence that these examples come from the US, for there is a much stronger tradition of general shareholder consciousness in that country than elsewhere. In the UK the level of active interest is far lower,[19] but there are signs of nascent interest. One such is the setting up of an Ethical Investment Research and Information Service (EIRIS). Aimed initially at individual shareholders, EIRIS is laying the basis for a development of alternative approaches which give some place to criteria other than that of direct economic return. Another is the Friends Provident Stewardship Trust, a unit trust committed to observing its clients' ethical principles in its investment policies but with a track record which shows an above average return on conventional economic criteria. Unity Trust is a trade-union-sponsored financial institution which concerns itself with domestic investment geared to the creation of jobs in the British economy and aims to draw on pension fund capital for this purpose. It celebrated its first birthday in 1985 with what the *Financial Times* called a 'modest but nonetheless tangible profit'. The TUC is beginning to promote initiatives along the lines adopted by its American counterpart, encouraging pension fund trustees to take an active interest in shaping investment criteria; it has, for example, appealed to union trustees on company pension funds to sell investments in ten named companies if they failed to reveal details of the conditions of black employees in South African subsidiaries (*Financial Times*, 9 April

1985). Several local authorities are considering the establishment of a Pensions Investment Resource Centre, to promote 'responsible investment policies and initiatives'. These would be geared to achieving rates of return through supporting real growth, taking into account the environmental, employment, social and economic effects of investment.

Finally, there have been moves to mobilise pension fund power against political initiatives which are seen as detrimental to scheme members – most notably the Conservative government's programme of privatisation. The success of the flotations depends heavily on the reaction of the financial institutions.[20] One response has been to argue that the pension funds of employees whose employment contracts would be affected by privatisation should actively resist it by proclaiming their intentions not to buy the floated shares (Locksley and Minns, 1984). So far this approach has not gathered effective support, but it is another sign of the growing entanglement of pension funds in the political economy of the UK.

Full treatment of the idea of 'alternative' investment strategies is well beyond the scope of this book. We have already strayed somewhat from the descriptive account of pension fund management with which this chapter has been primarily concerned. But one point requires emphasis. The adoption by capital-holders of 'alternative' criteria for investment may seem to imply a willingness to forego part of the economic returns which they could have expected if they had followed orthodox procedures. This may indeed be the case in certain instances, and be accepted as a price worth paying. But 'economic' and 'non-economic' objectives are not necessarily in opposition to each other. Non-economic considerations can be built into investment policy without impairing economic performance, as the example of the Friends Provident shows. Very thorny questions remain: what criteria are to be adopted? who is to decide on them? what techniques are to be used for assessing and evaluating investment projects? what is the role of the market to be? These and other pertinent questions are often skirted round by the proponents of alternative approaches. But the direct opposition between 'economic' and 'non-economic' approaches is a simplistic and unjustified antithesis.

Conclusion

In this chapter I have suggested that the growth of pension funds constitutes a significant shift in the pattern of ownership of British capital; that the power which derives from ownership was never clearcut and is certainly not made translucent by the emergence of institutional owners; and that the relationships of power between owners and managers at the level of the industrial enterprise have their counterparts at the level of the financial institution, the two levels being moreover closely intertwined. Overall, the member trustees – representing the nearest one can find to the 'owners' of the funds – may seem to be fairly tightly trussed as far as the control of capital is concerned. But the structural level of this analysis needs to be supplemented by a more close-up view of the process of pension fund management and the role and attitudes of the individuals involved.

Notes

1. Other countries base their pension systems on entirely different principles as regards both tax and savings: West Germany, for example, uses an insurance principle for its occupational pensions, allowing the capital to be retained within the company rather than being accumulated in a separate fund.
2. Arguably it has been the emergence of a vocal ecological movement which has brought a fresh dimension to thinking about the responsibilities of ownership. See Gorz (1985) for a trenchant critique of orthodox approaches to economic development on both left and right of the political spectrum.
3. For one approach to this, see Andrew (1981):

> Most languages distinguish ownership from possession in a manner similar to English (propriété – possession, Eigentum – Besitz) so that no linguistic absurdity exists with reference to a private possession being common property or publicly owned. Ownership connotes greater exclusivity than possession; what is one's own (eigen, propre or other Romance derivatives of the Latin proprius) inheres in *ownership*, Eigentum and propriété and not in possession or Besitz. Ownership pertains to the right to use and abuse, and the right to sell or otherwise alienate something, while possession pertains to a less absolute right to use, one which is subject to the conditions imposed by the lease. (1981, p. 67)

See also Scott (1982) and Thompson (1982) for criticisms of the common failure to use the concept of ownership with adequate care.
4. The *degree* of control is a continuous variable measuring the discretion which the controlling group has to pursue its own objectives; the authors relate this ultimately to voting power. *Location* covers the different forms of internal and external control, distinguishing amongst other things between individual and institutional shareholders as external controllers.
5. Useem provides a three-stage model which might be applied to the trends described so far in this chapter, referring mainly to the US but also to the UK: 'By the middle of this century, family capitalism had given way to managerial capitalism, and in recent decades managerial capitalism itself has been giving way to institutional capitalism' (1984, p. 16), though he rejects the view that managerial control reduced the drive to maximise profits. However, 'institutional' in the sense he uses it refers to large corporations as institutions, rather than to financial institutions as such.
6. Hirschman's typology of shareholder behaviour is useful. 'Exit' refers to the shareholder's freedom to take capital away from the company by selling stock, and 'voice' to the use of shareholder rights explicitly to influence company behaviour. 'Loyalty', on the other hand, is the more or less passive acceptance of existing practice (1970).
7. See especially the question of fund surpluses discussed in Chapter 3.
8. An anecdotal illustration was given to me by the pensions manager from an American drug company with a subsidiary in the UK. The parent company decided to take a closer interest in the pension funds of its subsidiaries, so it simply appointed three trustees who fly across the Atlantic for the board meetings, carrying headquarters'

instructions. No notification was given to the scheme's members, other than the appearance of all the trustees' names in the little-read annual report.
9. Useem quotes the president of a large American firm explaining that serving on the boards of other corporations helps him to make judgements on a range of policy areas: 'such things as strategic planning, personnel development, budgeting, internal controls, managing pension funds...' (1984, p. 47).
10. The role of insurance companies, which are estimated to manage about half of the total assets, is particularly in need of detailed analysis. This will be all the more true if the plans for portable pensions go through, as the consequent drainage of money from the pension funds would directly swell the sums under the management of the insurance companies.
11. Malcolm (1985). Mr Malcolm is chief investment manager of Royal Insurance.
12. See Useem (1984) and Whitley (1974). But the real power of this network may be exaggerated – see Pahl and Winkler (1974).
13. It is worth noting that in Canada it is forbidden for a bank to do both simultaneously.
14. The clients requiring briefing are not nervous small investors with no professional knowledge.

> Leading British finance directors remain largely ignorant of the alignments being formed by banks and stockbrokers in the City... Of 50 finance directors surveyed the most knowledgeable could name five only of the new City groupings and 18 could mention not even one. The survey implies that the City firms have largely failed to keep their big corporate clients informed of big changes in ownership and relationships. (*Financial Times*, 13 March 1985)

15. Following the Johnson Matthey Bank scandal in 1985, the Financial Times observed (in a leader titled 'Owners and Supervisors'): 'It is questionable whether institutional shareholders will ever be particularly effective chasers after productivity or second guessers of management strategy... Yet if there is any area where the institutions can exert effective pressure, it is precisely in relation to such things as standards of reporting, boardroom structure and audit committees... Had the institutional shareholders demanded better information on the sources of clearing banks' profits they might conceivably have done a service for management as well as for themselves.' (*Financial Times* 27 August 1985) Clive Thornton, former chief of Abbey National Building Society, went further, in a speech on the topic of the morality of wealth creation. Commenting on the dearth of bold and imaginative investment in British industry, he castigated the 'dull, unimaginative and unentrepreneurial' people for coming unprepared to board meetings – and for ignoring the social responsibility involved in shareholdership (*Financial Times*, 15 November 1984).
16. The examples confirm that it is public-sector funds that are at the forefront. It is worth noting that these actions are often carried out not by individual funds but by consortia, sometimes via the Investment Protection Committees organised by the National Association of Pension Funds. This is significant in that it illustrates something of the scope for collective action, rather than each fund acting in isolation to safeguard the interests only of its own members. This suggests a wider definition of obligation.
17. An alternative official policy might be to permit or even increase economic activity in South Africa on the grounds that this is the best way to promote the well-being of black Africans, especially if proper wages are paid. Both approaches, though irreconcilable, are based on ethical considerations rather than purely economic ones – though the stance taken may of course be hypocritical.
18. Interest in the adoption of social criteria is not confined to pension funds but extends to other financial institutions such as unit trusts. One example is Working Assets, a California-based unit trust which advertises itself with a picture of US missiles jutting into the sky over the following caption: 'It's 11 p.m. Do you know where your money is? Working Assets won't use your money to finance nuclear overkill.'

19. It may be that this will be changed by the intense publicity given to the selling off of public assets in the name of shareholder democracy, as well as the fiscal and ideological promotion of profit-sharing schemes. It would be something of an irony if this enhanced awareness of capital ownership were to lead to the exercise of ownership rights along distinctively non-capitalist lines.
20. Even where there is a substantial take-up of shares by individuals, most of them find their way quickly to the institutions as individuals take their profit and sell on.

6 The Impact of Member Representation

Judgement of the value and effect of participation involves a whole range of considerations. In the first place, participation may simply be valued for itself: it is the sign of a maturing democracy that greater rights are accorded to a wider segment of the population, regardless of how those rights are exercised. In view of how recently representation has been introduced for the most part, it might be thought unrealistic to expect many very concrete results. On the other hand, some (often rather ingenuous) accounts of participation in other areas report immediate and tangible effects, for example on industrial relations or worker satisfaction. Productivity goes up, labour turnover goes down and the parties concerned pronounce themselves happy, or at least happier than they were before. In the more theoretical approaches there is often an assumption that greater democracy brings wider benefits - for example that workers' control at company level will make socialised planning of the economy a smoother and more rational affair. I do not wish to throw positivist cold water over these assumptions by insisting on hard evidence for the benefits of participation. Nor do I subscribe to the approach which focusses invariably on the negative aspects or limitations of any initiative. A more detailed look at the outcomes - so far as we can discern them - should help to do two things. It should illuminate the constraints which operate on the extent to which representation has had and can have an impact; and it should clarify the often implicit and sometimes conflicting goals which it is supposed to achieve.

What is expected of member trustees, and by whom? Is participation pointless unless they immediately assert themselves over the direction of the capital under their trust? If there is no apparent change in the behaviour of the fund, or in the administration of the scheme, does this mean that the member trustees have been incorporated into the system, subverted by the occasional City lunch? How quickly can they be expected to make an impact? All these are legitimate questions, to which the following pages supply no clearcut answer. In analysing the nature of trustee participation I draw rather more than hitherto on case study evidence for insight and illustration. The case studies are not representative of pension schemes as a whole, being drawn mainly from larger companies and all having member trustees or other substantial forms of participation (see Appendix). It might have been illuminating to interview managers in organisations with no participation, to see for example whether they rejected the notion of pensions as deferred pay and therefore saw no rationale for member involvement. But it is natural – in the first instance at any rate – to mine richer seams from which lessons for the future can be learnt.

Chapter 4, presented a classification of trustee activities. This is not definitive and there is a fair degree of variety in the extent to which trustee boards engage in each or all of the activities, but it was generally recognised by respondents as a meaningful summary of their functions. The first task is to give some sort of differential weighting to the activities since it would be wrong to assume that they all have the same significance. Pensions managers and member trustees were asked to rank trustee activities in order of importance. The results are given in Table 6.1.

Table 6.1: Rankings of trustee activities (pensions manager and member trustee surveys)

Percentage of respondents choosing (a) as first priority
(b) as first or second priority

	Pension managers (a)	Pension managers (b)	Member trustees (a)	Member trustees (b)
Dissemination of information	5	19	15	27
Exercise of discretionary powers	13	26	13	24
Investment policy	43	66	31	54
Monitoring fund performance	8	33	25	56
Application and changes of rules	17	27	13	27
Selection of advisers/managers	14	30	3	11
	100%		100%	

There is a clear consensus on the primacy of investment policy as the most important function of the trustees. 'Policy' is of course a fuzzy term. It can be interpreted in a loose sense as the observance of broad guidelines only, with maximum discretion being left to the investment managers, internal or external. Trustees may be content to secure themselves legally by relying wholly on professional expertise on a very slack rein. Or they may take a more active interest, initiating shifts in the proportions to be allocated to different sectors and listening carefully to information offered on the prospects for investment in different markets. It would be wrong to identify interest in detail with strength of policy control, as the venerable distinction between strategy and tactics suggests. The central feature is the general responsibility for the scheme's assets.

Pensions managers put investment policy substantially further out in front than member trustees. In part this derives from a stronger allegiance to the company, especially since pressure on the company to maintain or raise its contribution levels will vary according to the performance of the funds. The more profitably the assets are handled, the less the company is likely to have to put in to produce a given level of pension – although the extent of its ability to benefit in this way is a reflection of routine practice and power, and not of formal rights: the fruits of good performance are in principle just as eligible for distribution to existing pensioners and to current employees, in the form of improved benefits or reduced contributions, as they are for retention by the company. The gap between the priorities of managers and member trustees is closed if the monitoring performance function is bracketed with investment policy under the more general rubric of financial control. The fact that member trustees rate monitoring nearly as high as investment policy reflects a combination of two factors: awareness of the limitations of their own influence on the latter and a live appreciation of the paramountcy of financial considerations. Member trustees know that the handling of the assets is crucial but they are conscious of the fact that their role in this is largely restricted to the retrospective vetting and approval of what has been done.

On two of the other activities there is no significant difference in the judgements of managers and member trustees: the exercise of discretionary powers and the application and changes of rules are both given relatively low priorities. Views on the dissemination of information, however, diverge quite sharply. For member trustees it is the third most important activity whilst managers rate it lowest of all. This shows clearly that for member trustees the point of reference is, understandably, their own role as distinct from that of trustees as a whole. It underlines an anomaly pointed to earlier (Chapter 4): under law trustees all have the same obligations, but in practice there is a division of labour with member trustees being expected to concentrate more on acting as the eyes and ears of the scheme members. They naturally give a higher priority to the function in which they are themselves most actively involved. By contrast the selection of advisers and managers appears almost irrelevant for member trustees. As we shall see, this correlates closely with their low level of involvement in this activity. Managers, on the other hand, give a much higher ranking to choosing – and confirming the choice of – professional financial expertise.

Another angle on trustee activities is provided by the responses to a question in both surveys which asked respondents whether trustee boards mainly initiated decisions in the different areas or mainly ratified proposals put to them. The distinction is a fairly crude one, but the results confirm the picture which is beginning to emerge. (See Table 6.2.)

Table 6.2: Do trustee boards ratify or initiate decisions? *(pensions manager and member trustee surveys)*

Percentages. Answers do not total 100 per cent where not all respondents replied.

	Pension managers Ratify	Pension managers Initiate	Member trustees Ratify	Member trustees Initiate
Dissemination of information	46	41	43	54
Exercise of discretionary powers	39	48	47	49
Investment policy	38	45	67	29
Monitoring fund performance	43	40	59	39
Application and changes of rules	46	40	53	46
Selection of advisers/managers	33	51	44	50

Two significant differences emerge. Pensions managers see the board as taking far more initiative on investment policy than do member trustees; and the converse is true, to a lesser degree, on the dissemination of information. It is worth noting that on this question there is no emphasis in the member trustee replies on an active role in monitoring to compensate for passivity over investment policy.

Member Trustees: Their Contribution and Effect

We now turn specifically to the role played by member trustees. What are the advantages, and disadvantages, of member participation? Evidence given to the Occupational Pensions Board for its 1982 Report fell under the following headings. The perceived advantages were improved staff relations, with less suspicion and a greater feeling of security and justice; greater member appreciation of the value of the scheme; better communications between scheme managers and members; more informed input into the exercise of discretionary powers; the opportunity for members to influence benefits and make recommendations on priorities; and the opportunity for members to influence investment policy. Possible disadvantages included lack of experience and expertise on the part of member representatives; loss of efficiency and time; extra expense to employers; problems of confidentiality; and the difficulty of representing retired members (OPB 1982, pp. 185-7). We look first at the evidence on what sort of impact member trustees were seen to have made, and then at judgements on the value of their contributions.

Table 6.3: Contribution of member trustees to trustee board activities (as reported by pensions managers (PM), member trustees (MT) and case study interviewees (CS))

Reported level of contribution (%)

	High			Medium			Low			None		
	PM	MT	CS	PM	MT	CS	PM	MT	CS	PM	MT	CS
Dissemination of information	55	57	58	31	33	19	10	7	16	3	3	6
Exercise of discretionary powers	43	45	50	40	39	18	13	12	20	3	4	11
Monitoring of fund performance	11	33	29	40	41	32	36	21	35	12	5	4
Application and changes of rules	27	31	35	45	41	27	22	18	26	6	10	12
Investment policy	18	17	18	37	34	27	33	35	30	12	14	15
Appointment of managers/advisers	16	11	19	21	24	21	36	37	27	26	28	32

Table 6.3 presents the assessments made by the respondents of the contributions made by member trustees (as distinct from trustees generally) to each of the activities. Included here are the views of all the case study respondents, who constitute a mixture of managers, company-appointed trustees, member trustees and others involved in pensions decision-making such as personnel directors. The activities are listed in descending order according to the member trustees' perceptions of their own level of contribution. The most obvious result is the unanimity amongst all categories of respondent on dissemination of information as the activity in which member trustees are most heavily involved. There is a similar total agreement on the exercise of discretionary powers in second place and virtual unanimity on the appointment of advisers as the function where member trustees make least contribution of all.

The only significant divergence in assessment is over the monitoring of fund performance. One-third of member trustees reckoned that they make a high contribution to this, and only a quarter that they make a low contribution or none at all. By contrast only 11 per cent of managers assess the contribution as high, and almost half think that member trustees make no or little contribution. (The pot is, of course, half full as well as half empty: over 50 per cent of managers rate the member trustee contribution as high or medium.) The difference is at least partly explicable if we remember the primacy of the finance-related functions. Since member trustees make little claim to have much of a role in the fashioning of investment policy, they will be inclined to register activity on the monitoring side. Otherwise they are acknowledging exclusion from the most significant areas of decision-making.

In presenting the responses given to a question about the level of member trustees' contribution to the different activities, Table 6.3 contains some ambiguity. Some respondents may have compared the member trustees' contributions in one area with their contributions in another, whilst others rated them in absolute terms or compared their contributions with those of company trustees or other personnel in the same area. The different judgements would not then be incompatible: member trustees feel that they contribute highly to monitoring because they compare it with their contribution to, say, investment policy, whilst pensions managers see the contribution as low because they compare member trustees' contributions to that of other trustees or outside influences. The absence of a single explicit reference point means that the data do not yield absolute quantitative comparisons. It is nevertheless firmly indicative of a particular pattern, and a fairly clearcut polarisation emerges. The role of member trustees is primarily to handle issues which relate to individual members as recipients of information or as agents affected by the use of discretionary powers. These functions may, to be sure, involve decisions which can reasonably be said to have strategic implications. For example, decisions about how much information is to be distributed, and to whom, have obvious implications for the accountability of fund management. The exercise of discretionary powers also involves decisions which by setting a precedent go beyond the particular instance and into the realm of policy. Nevertheless the two functions deal directly primarily with individual scheme members. The more effective member trustees are, the better informed will members be about their own benefit positions and the fairer discretionary decisions are likely to be. By contrast the areas of decision-making which affect the scheme as a whole, and which are identified by all parties as of primary importance, are those to which member trustees apparently make least contribution – in particular, investment policy.

What effect do these contributions have? A general question in both surveys asked respondents whether they felt there had been an improvement or deterioration in a number of areas as a result of participation. The question did not explicitly restrict the interpretation of participation to the presence of member trustees, and this largely explains why so many more member trustees (63 per cent) than pensions managers (14 per cent) reported an improvement in benefit levels: member trustees will have been more likely to include negotiations in their interpretation. Broadly speaking the reponses to the question confirmed the previous pattern. Improvements in member awareness and the quality of information were reported by over four-fifths of the member trustees and about two-thirds of the pensions managers. Investment performance, on the other hand, was seen as unchanged by 64 per cent and 95 per cent of the respondents respectively. Two further points emerged. First, whether or not participation resulted directly in improvement in benefit levels it was widely judged to have raised the status of pensions within the company, making it easier for those involved in pensions decisions to argue their case for improvements, whether with fellow-managers or fellow-trade unionists and scheme members. Secondly, improvements in industrial relations generally as a consequence of pensions participation were recorded by over half the pensions managers and almost three-quarters of the member trustees. These responses are obviously subjective and the causality is uncertain: participation may be the product as much as the cause of better industrial relations. But the positive judgements of effect were widespread.

The most common overall assessment of the input of member trustees was a loose one: that it was difficult to specify the effect precisely, but that participation had been generally positive. It was certainly the case that even where participation had so far had little tangible impact, there were hardly any positive disadvantages recorded. Even the more jaundiced participants did not advocate a withdrawal, as has been the experience in other forums where participation has been apparently ineffective. But there is more to say than this rather back-handed compliment.

Chapter 4 outlined a number of factors involved in the growth of participation at trustee level. It was clear that the actual initiative had almost invariably been taken by management. Typical of this was the response of a personnel director to the question of why participation had been introduced: 'From the company's point of view, to ensure that we took the initiative in an area of vital interest, at the forefront of politics and economics.' In some cases the reasoning was more negative, to head off the prospect that pensions would be brought into the negotiating arena, though as we have seen there is a divergence of managerial strategy on this score, with some companies actively seeking to include pensions in the total bargaining package. A common sentiment was that pensions decision-making at trustee level was an area of consensus in which all participants shared a common interest, so that the inclusion of member trustees would be relatively risk-free for the company. It is doubtful, however, whether expectations about the impact of member representation have often been clearly defined beforehand.

To management the chief advantage has been twofold. First is the increased credibility which member participation gives to the scheme, regardless of the material impact. The simple existence of member trustees seems to reassure members that their interests are being safeguarded 'however trivial the involvement', as one pensions manager put it. Secondly, and relatedly, is an improvement in the flow of information, both upwards and downwards:

> It allows the company to be more informative to the members. It's useful to Charles [the investment manager] to see the reactions of the employee representatives on the trustee board in gauging how to get the message across. It helps them to see and hear the investment manager, not just as some shadowy figure. (A personnel manager)

and 'It gives management much better insight into the relative priorities of all potential recipients (even between past and present employees), to the point of being able to delegate the responsibility for the balance to the employee representatives' (a pensions manager).

Member trustees encountered some of the problems familiar to many involved in any form of representative decision-making, especially when it occurs away from the place of work: 'People tend to distrust you when you spend two or three days away. How do you get across to your fellow-workers that you're always on their side?' and 'Being seen to be party to a decision which is not acceptable, you sometimes get a bit of stick. Almost inadvertently you defend the damned thing. Having more information is often difficult.' (Quotations are from member trustees, except where otherwise specified).

Expectations may be high compared with what can be delivered: 'Lay members probably think we have more power than we have.' On the other hand the counterpart to improved credibility is the opportunity afforded for generating greater interest in pensions, both amongst members and amongst union representatives. In the latter case, it has also led to the accumulation of some expertise on pensions as a potentially negotiable item: 'We've been able to create an awareness amongst our members of the importance of pensions. And there are now some people, including those who sit on the Management Committee [a consultative body] who know about pensions.' Enhanced familiarity and interest feed back into the bargaining process at different levels.

But the development of expertise amongst the member trustees themselves is also seen as a significant outcome. The notion of participation as itself an educative process has a long tradition, stretching back to J.S. Mill. It is inevitably not something that occurs overnight, but it can in the longer term lead on to further initiatives with implications that go beyond the single scheme:

> We've been able to involve ourselves and develop experience which we've brought to the union movement as a whole. By our own pressures and picking the right staff, we've been able to initiate work on a whole range of things, such as what is risk, how to measure it, and so on. And we've been able to raise issues such as South Africa and thalidomide. We've been able to create an ethos in the way things are run.

This last quotation is without doubt exceptional in the degree of confidence and sophistication it exhibits. The individual in question was a trustee in a scheme which has had participation for longer than most; he was, moreover, a union official who brought to his position as trustee a wealth of experience as a negotiator and a member of other significant bodies. The scheme in question is one of the largest in the country, with considerable resources of management expertise. Nevertheless in a longer-term perspective the points he makes are significant for the future role of trustees generally, as their collective experience accumulates.

On *investment*, there are no 'hard' indicators of the extent of member trustee influence in terms of measurable changes in the funds' policies. The evidence is qualitative and relies on the perceptions of individuals, involving a number of different types of influence. The first distinction is between *intermittent* and *continuous* influence. Particular instances of member trustees making a significant contribution can be illuminating. Occasionally a member trustee would recount with pride how he had opposed the viewpoint of a professional adviser in a discussion of where to invest new income. These are the instances which understandably stick in the respondent's memory. But given the consensual nature of trustee decision-making, influence cannot be adequately identified by reference to the winning of particular disputes. Moreover, individual decisions need to be distinguished from strategic policy-making. Indeed, member trustees who recounted instances of this kind were on the whole less likely to exhibit an interest in strategic policy issues. More significant is the sort of influence which is exercised evenly and continuously, without being dependent on particular trials of strength. One respondent observed that he could not pinpoint particular instances of member trustees influencing decisions, but described the impact of their presence as follows: 'Employee representatives have a watchdog role – it keeps management on their toes and makes them ask, "What are the buggers going to ask today?"'

Necessarily such influence is often exercised *implicitly* rather than explicitly. This is by no means to downgrade it; power which is exercised unperceived is more firmly secure than that which has to be openly asserted and reasserted. An investment manager described how the investment committee of his board acts as a constraint because it means that he simply does not propose policies which he thinks they will disagree with. Such influence may not be evident even to those who exercise it: a member trustee in a different scheme explained the limitations which he perceived on his own effectiveness, but also described how, needled by these limitations, he had asked the chairman of his trustee board why the company bothered to allow the presence of member trustees. 'He replied – and convinced me – that our presence makes them [the professionals] prepare explanations. The expert has to explain things to the novice, and that's useful.' I return to the question of expertise later.

Thirdly, and again relatedly, there is a distinction between a contribution in the form of a positive suggestion or *initiative*, and the *reactive* mode of influence. One member trustee, convinced that not enough venture capital is made available for new enterprises, takes the initiative in proposing each year that his scheme should write to the top 1000 pension funds suggesting that they get together and allocate up to 2 per cent into high risk investment. His proposal is regularly blocked by everyone else, including the other member trustees, and has not (yet) succeeded; whether or not this would be regarded as a valid contribution is a matter of judgement, but he has at least taken the initiative in raising an issue and proposing a line of action. Again, however, it would be a mistake to downgrade reactive behaviour as a less significant form of potential influence. In the case study where member trustees (in this case, union officials from outside the scheme) carried on almost any definition the greatest weight the Chief Executive explained that there was no question of the trustees originating any proposals. He formulates them himself – but unlike his counterpart referred to earlier he positively expects challenges and disagreements: 'Of course. On about one in every ten issues. If not, there's something wrong.' Indeed, he regards it as part of his job to make sure that the trustees are well enough informed so that constructive argument takes place and 'we can disagree in the way that all intelligent people should'.

This illustrates well how the nature of the member trustee contributions depends on the social climate within the board, and more broadly within the company itself. The existence of member trustees suggests a generally more 'progressive' personnel policy, yet it covers an enormous range of attitudes. In some cases member trustees are made to feel that they are present only on sufferance. This shapes their attitude and the nature of their interventions, and is often a reflection of the overall tenor of industrial relations. In others there is a climate of collaboration which is acknowledged and accepted even where the member trustees are experienced union representatives used to tough negotiations in the collective bargaining field. Opposition certainly occurs, and may even be drawn up on familiar lines, with management and member trustees on different sides. But a trustee with impeccable negotiating credentials observed that in his experience traditional political attitudes and alliances were often inappropriate in the context of the trustee board. He added:

> That may sound as if I've been sucked into the system. I have noticed that there is often an alignment between the externally-appointed other trustees (i.e. bankers) and the union trustees against the internal company trustees – so we line up with the arch capitalists!

The alignments to which he referred were evidently not of the same order as orthodox bargaining postures.

Not surprisingly, there is more specific evidence demonstrating an association between the presence of member trustees and different practices on *information dissemination*. Information about pension schemes has been a source of recurrent concern. In 1982 the Occupational Pensions Board, in a report dealing with greater security for the rights and expectations of members, noted that none of its 1975 report's proposals for mandatory disclosure requirements had been adopted. It reaffirmed its doubt that voluntary disclosure is 'ever likely to be extensive enough, either in the information disclosed or the number of schemes involved, to provide adequately for the needs of all scheme members' (1982, p. 37). A 1984 survey of information provision by over 400 schemes, carried out by the British Institute of Management (BIM), concluded bluntly: 'Clearly standards are going to have to improve.' Of the 250 schemes that published reports, less than one-fifth included the 'very important' borrowings statement, crucial to an understanding of the scheme's liabilities. 'Equally noteworthy, less than one third (31%) included a statement of investments exceeding 5% [of the total assets]; even the auditor's report was included by less than half the publishers' (BIM, 1984, p. 26).

The provision of information is not restricted to the distribution of paper. Some schemes have highly developed consultative structures and, at plant level, pensions representatives whose function it is to advise individuals personally. But member trustees, especially in big organisations, cannot hope to undertake the transmission of information directly themselves, so their impact must mainly be on its distribution. Table 6.4 presents evidence from the pensions manager survey on the general pattern of provision in this respect, and on the contrast between companies with member trustees and those without.

Table 6.4: Availability of information (pensions manager survey)

(a) All schemes %
(b) Distinguishing between schemes with and without member trustees (MT) (%)

	(a) All schemes			(b) Schemes where information automatically available	
	Auto- matically	On request	Not at all	With MTs	Without MTs
Detailed rules	22	70	8	22	22
Trust deed	3	89	7	3	3
Annual reports	54	36	10	70	33
Actuary's report	12	55	33	17	8
Investment details	11	56	33	18	5
Explanatory booklet	92	6	2	100	84
Individual benefit statement	65	32	3	78	53

There are two points to be drawn out. First, the presence of member trustees coincides with a markedly greater propensity to make information available on an automatic basis. Four out of five organisations with member trustees give their members an individual benefit statement automatically, compared with just over half of those without member trustees. Proportionately over twice as many provide annual reports on the scheme. Of greater significance in the context of economic democracy is the contrast in the provision of a breakdown of the fund's investments: nearly one in five organisations with member trustees furnishes such details to its members without them asking for it, but only one in twenty where there is no representation.[1] If access to knowledge generally is one of the building blocks of democracy, then distribution of information on where the funds are placed is a necessary step towards economic democracy. It is not surprising to see it sitting alongside member representation.

I have avoided attributing this generosity of information directly to the presence of member trustees. Coincidence, we know, is not causality. It is the larger organisations which tend to have member trustees: they will also be more likely to find it cost-effective to distribute information widely and anyway to have a more developed personnel function which encourages more open communication. So participation may just be one of a bundle of associated characteristics and we cannot conclude that the member trustees have been themselves responsible for an upsurge of information: the association is still worth signalling.

Secondly Table 6.4 shows variations in the pattern of access to different items of information, with explanatory booklets and individual benefit statements being far more commonly available than the actuary's report or investment details.[2] It is not surprising that the former are so widely distributed. Indeed the only puzzling thing on these items is how the 3 per cent of companies who do not make benefit statements available to individuals even on request justify their practice – perhaps on the grounds that it is nice to have a little surprise when you retire. It is also predictable that the actuary's report and investment details are not usually provided on an automatic basis. Most people, after all, are primarily interested in understanding what their own position is, and excessive information, especially in legal jargon, would be a waste of paper. It is, however, significant that on both items in about one-third of the cases the information is not available even if the member is interested enough to request it. In some cases this may be because the facts are genuinely not available, for example where the fund is fully insured and its assets pooled along with many others in an insurance company. In other cases they are not available only because it has never been the practice to prepare them for distribution, and not for any intrinsic reason. The 1982 OPB Report, whilst recognising that valuation reports and trust deeds are bulky documents which it would not be economical to distribute widely, recommended that they should be made available for inspection at the principal place of employment by any scheme member or union representative. It also recommended that a summary description of scheme assets should be included in the annual report, including insurance policies and drawing attention to any concentrations of investment (especially self-investment) amounting to over 10 per cent of the scheme's assets. Actuaries' reports in their current form are hardly the most digestible reading, but there seems little reason why they should only be composed for an exclusively professional audience.³ And it is, to say the least, odd that the putative owners of the assets should not have access to the form their assets take.

More importantly, the two items in question – investment details and the actuary's report – are precisely those that cover the strategic management of the fund. In short, we find in the distribution of information the same pattern as we found in the activities of member trustees: *a concentration on issues which concern individual employees and a general abstinence from involvement in the strategy of capital allocation.* One can go further. This pattern reproduces the divide referred to previously in the overall character of the occupational pensions system. On the one hand we have a concern with the management of age, through the administration of benefits, and on the other with the management of capital in the shape of the funds themselves. The cleavage penetrates right down to the distribution of information, and underlies many of the ambiguities in the minds of both managers and trustees over the control of the schemes.

Further confirmation of this division is to be found in the ranking and level of member trustee contribution to the *appointment of advisers*. Chapter 5 described the key role which advisers have in the management of assets, but their selection is an activity which barely impinges on most trustees: the advisers were there when they arrived on the board, and though there may be the occasional change of merchant bank, it is almost invariably seen as a decision to be taken by the company rather than the board of trustees. As the competition for pension fund business hots up, it is probable that the issue of adviser selection will receive more attention from trustees. Partly this will stem from the increased marketing efforts of rival institutions, especially those trying to break into a market whose lucrative potential is now very evident. This will be further encouraged by the shake-up currently taking place within the City as a whole. It will also happen as trustees look more carefully at their own procedures for monitoring costs and performance, and at the likelihood that they will themselves be subject to closer scrutiny over their stewardship of the assets. They will therefore be looking, on the financial side, for advisers who can deliver the best value for money (on which there is remarkably little solid information). But there is another factor. Trustees can defend themselves at law from the charge of dereliction of duty by showing that they followed the counsel of professional advisers. Not all advisers will take the same view of, for example, the riskiness of a given project or approach, so trustees who have their own, perhaps unorthodox, ideas about investment policy may begin to look for advisers who will broadly share their viewpoint. There need be nothing conspiratorial about this; it is the pension fund equivalent of a closer working relationship between providers of capital and managers of industrial enterprises. But the fact that the present member trustees both rate the function so low and make so little contribution to it is an indication of the independence which company managements at present have in this area.

This is confirmed by Table 6.5, which gives the views of all the case study respondents when asked to identify the most important agents in each of the trustee functions. It confirms the difference between investment decisions and their monitoring discussed earlier, with the investment manager and the trustees (including company trustees) switching places. It puts the contribution of member trustees into some perspective, since even in the area where they make most contribution – information dissemination – it is the pensions manager who is rated by far the most important single influence. The one area where joint management–employee bodies dominate is the exercise of discretionary powers: if it is not the trustees it is a management committee which may either be a subsidiary of the board or an independent body in which there is likely to be member participation. In the first five areas, it is noticeable that all the agents identified are internal to the scheme.[4] But on the appointment of advisers it is company management, that is executives who have no formal role within the scheme itself, that are the key influence. This finding should be related back to Figure 5.1, where it illustrates forcefully the significance of line 5.

Table 6.5: Perceived key agents in trustee functions (case study respondents)

Trustee function	Identified key influence	(% of respondents)	2nd most commonly identified	(%)
Dissemination of information	Pensions manager	(36)	All trustees	(18)
Exercise of discretionary powers	All trustees	(31)	Management committee	(14)
Investment policy	Investment manager (internal)	(31)	All trustees	(18)
Monitoring of fund performance	All trustees	(32)	Investment manager	(20)
Application and changes of rules	Pensions manager	(27)	All trustees	(18)
Appointment of managers/ advisers	Company management	(37)	All trustees	(25)

Constraints on Member Trustees

I turn now to deal in detail with the constraints which operate on member trustees, but these should not be read in a purely negative light. Not only is the identification of constraints a necessary condition of increasing the effectiveness of member trustees, but the constraints are in any case not absolute. It should already be clear that the process of pensions decision-making, especially on the capital management side, is complex and takes place within a broader framework of financial practices. Quite apart from everything else, the sheer bulk of the schemes is such that it would take time to turn the tanker even with a hard wrench on the tiller. One must not exaggerate this, nor the necessary complexity of fund management. Nevertheless since it appears that the effect of the increased presence of member trustees has been largely confined to the more personnel-oriented areas, and since all those involved agree that financial strategy is the most important function of trustees, we must probe a little further.

First, one cannot assume that the lack of a clearly discernible impact means that there is no involvement. Most member trustees find little to criticise in their fund's investment policy, and their influence may be imperceptible simply because they have weighed up the issue fully and decided that there is no new contribution for them to make. Or they may positively throw their weight behind a confirmation of existing policy. Most expressed satisfaction with the way their own fund is handled. Only about one in ten of the case study interviewees had ever disagreed with an investment decision, and this had almost always been a one-off event. On the other hand, a much higher number expressed some unease about the role of the funds but felt unable to formulate specific alternative proposals. And a significant number of trustees frankly acknowledged that they were unable even to describe their fund's investment policy as such. Even if there had been total positive endorsement of current practice, it would still be worth reflecting on the reasons for such concurrence.

The analysis which follows refers far more to fund management than to other activities I have described. This is partly because of our focus on economic democracy, as the financial functions are identified by the participants themselves as of prime importance. But in any case the question of capital management presents the issues in their starkest form; many of the points apply also, if less forcefully, to member participation in the other areas.

1. Structural constraints
Formal exclusion
The simplest way of pre-empting member trustee influence is to exclude them from the bodies where decisions are made. This is perhaps the commonest overall complaint made against participation and consultative schemes in industry generally that decisions are taken outside

the participative body, and that there is no way of ensuring that the views expressed elsewhere carry any weight in the final assessment.

There are a number of variants on this theme, some of them peculiar to pension scheme management. The most clearcut organisational barrier is when a separate company is set up to handle the fund's assets, independent of the trustee board and with no employee representation. In one case study a member trustee explained that the employers had set up just such a company to handle the property side of the fund, buying and renting out buildings. He did not, however, refer to and might not even have been aware of the existence of a second company which handled the equities. He was certainly in no doubt about the limitations on his influence: 'All investment is left to four merchant banks and we were told in no uncertain terms that we have no right to influence this...The [company] trustees have a pre-meeting before the trustee meeting so everything is cut and dried.' He added wryly that similar things happen in negotiations, but there he can do something to change it, whereas in the trustee board he has no sanction to apply. The picture was confirmed by a company-appointed trustee (the company solicitor) in the same organisation; asked whether there were any disadvantages to member trusteeship, he replied: 'As we have constituted the arrangements, no; all responsibility for investment is delegated to another company. If we hadn't done that we would have had to discuss all the decisions on investments which could have been difficult.'

Other instances of exclusion were much less blatant in their motivation. One organisation had separate staff and manual schemes each with 50 per cent member representation, but a common investment committee. It allowed participation in the investment committee on a minority and rotating basis: two member trustees would attend each committee meeting, so the same trustee would not reappear again before at least a year had elapsed. This helped a little to familiarise member trustees with investment procedures and there was no attempt to conceal the structure, but clearly such a system of intermittent participation is not designed to foster direct member influence.

For a parallel we can turn to analyses of the structure of regular company boards. Both Batstone (1976) and Brookes (1979) refer to the setting up of sub-committees of the kind we commonly find in pension schemes dealing with investment. Batstone is firmly of the view that power drains away from the body on which there is employee representation – obeying, as it were, some law of anti-participatory gravity. The examples cited above tend to confirm this; on the other hand there are also instances of equal participation in the subsidiary committees, in line with Brookes' more ambivalent conclusions. In any case, organisational charts on their own are a poor guide to the relative powers of different organs. The investment sub-committee may itself be tightly constrained by guidelines laid down by the main board, or personal factors may intervene: in the example of rotating participation referred to above the Chairman of the Investment Committee is noted for his hostility to the principle of member trusteeship, and is powerfully placed to keep member representatives present very much on the sidelines.

Legal obligations and the pension fund system

I have referred earlier to the requirements imposed on trustees by trust law and the general obligation to act in the best interests of all the beneficiaries. I shall focus here on the member trustees' *perceptions* of the extent to which they are constrained by legal obligations, whether or not those perceptions are based, and continue to be based, on a correct interpretation of the law.

The perceptions form a spectrum. But in spite of the width of the spectrum, it should be made clear that there was not a single instance of a member trustee wishing to divest himself of his primary obligation to scheme members. The divergences are all matters of interpretation as to how this is best achieved. At one end are those who see the legal position as compelling them to rely entirely on professional advisers, and investment as a purely technical affair. Indeed 'doing one's best by the members' is literally to be equated with following current investment practice; although the professionals may not hit the bull's-eye on each and every investment, they are by definition the people by whose standards performance is to be judged. Not only, therefore, is a trustee absolutely safe from the legal point of view if he relies implicitly on their advice, it is also in fact the most effective way of deploying the assets. The simplest expression of this viewpoint was as follows: 'The thing is to provide adequate pensions. I have never thought about any other objective.' Others displayed an awareness that the role of the funds in the economy had been questioned and alternative approaches suggested, but were equally unequivocal that existing practice and criteria were entirely adequate. Notions of 'best return' and 'acceptable risk' were treated as non-problematic. But there was a range of other views, which recognised in varying degrees challenges to the role of the funds as institutional shareholders, with consequent implications for trustee responsibilities. Figure 6.1 allows us to explore these perceptions further, though the boxes are not to be taken as watertight.

Box 1 in Figure 6.1, then, contains the views referred to previously: that there are no legitimate grounds for debate. Box 2 is filled by people who felt that the situation had changed because of the growth of the funds, but implicitly or explicitly acknowledged that they were at a loss to know what the implications of this were. Typical of such views were 'It's so complex that I'm never quite sure which approach to take' and 'They

Figure 6.1: Does the size of pension funds affect their responsibilities as investors?

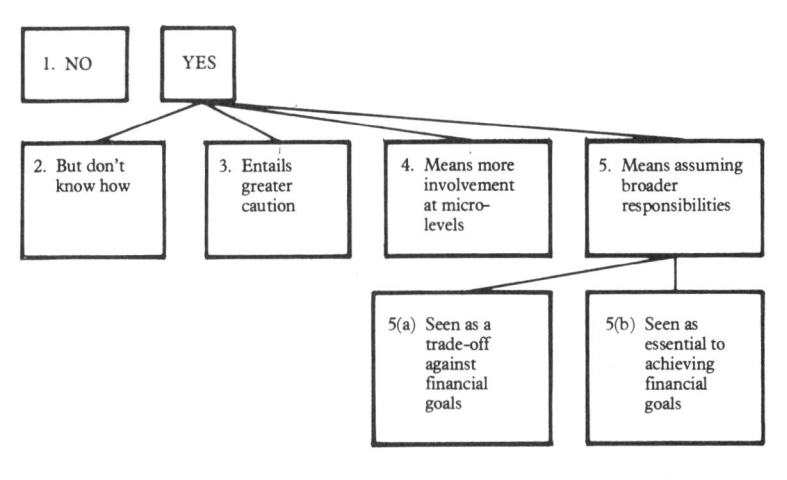

```
1. NO     YES
          ├──────────┬──────────────┬──────────────┐
2. But don't   3. Entails      4. Means more    5. Means assuming
   know how      greater          involvement      broader
                 caution          at micro-        responsibilities
                                  levels
                                           ┌──────────────┬──────────────┐
                                        5(a) Seen as a      5(b) Seen as
                                             trade-off           essential to
                                             against             achieving
                                             financial           financial
                                             goals               goals
```

[the funds] are becoming a dominant voice in the market, and this aspect has not been thought through...It's a hell of a power, and means that the responsibilities are much greater than when the [trustee] law was introduced' (company trustee).

Where implications were drawn, it was by no means always along the same lines. Some trustees inferred that the increase in their responsibility obliged them to shift further towards risk avoidance, since so much more now depended upon them (box 3). But this in turn raises the question of how to avoid risks – which was sometimes solved with the aid of hindsight:

> So much of the wealth of the country is concentrated in pension funds that they must behave responsibly. They shouldn't put money into things like Brighton Marina – highly speculative ventures which are likely to go wrong. Now if Clive Sinclair was in trouble that would be a different matter – I was only reading the other day in *Personal Computer* that he is bringing out another ZX mini-computer. [This was before the launch of the ill-fated C5 electric tricycle and Sinclair's subsequent problems.]

Plender (1982) provides several examples of how inconsistent is the attitude to risk-taking amongst fund managers, with investment in foreign property markets treated very differently to domestic investment. With the pundits of modern portfolio theory coming up with widely divergent answers, even when operating a narrowly defined framework of political economy, it is not surprising that trustees find it hard to pin down the notion of risk.

Box 4 refers to the issues discussed in the previous chapter and contains the views of those who were concerned about the relationship between company management and the funds as institutional shareholders. Two principal lines of thinking emerged. There were those who were critical of the way most companies are run, and felt that it was part of their responsibility to bring pressure to bear for changes in this respect. Others recognised the growing importance of the institutional shareholder but were uncertain about the degree of active intervention to be exercised. On the whole a closer relationship was anticipated, with the funds taking an active part in setting British industry to rights at this micro-level: 'I would like to see them exercise more power. Many individuals run their companies like private shows. It's hogwash about "first responsibility is to the shareholders". Because they have longer-term responsibilities, funds can force management to take a more strategic line.' A company trustee was more hesitant:

> The power of the institutional investor and when he should exercise that power is quite a problem. The ability of companies to talk with institutional investors is improving, but it's also a problem as they shouldn't talk to some shareholders and not to others. How does one get to know about a Rolls Royce situation, and what does one do about it?

Contrasting with these views was a set of concerns about the more general impact of the funds' collective weight on the economy. The relationship between conventional investment practice and possible alternative practice was seen as a legitimate issue for reflection, not because of an absolute opposition to the former but as a reflection of concern at the instability created by the growth of the funds as a whole. 'Structural' is an over-worked term but in this case it is apposite, for it denotes tension perceived between the obligations and traditions of schemes acting on an individual basis and the effect of their massive collective presence and behaviour.

The concern, however, took two fundamentally different forms. The first (box 5(a)) interprets the issue in terms of a *trade-off* which has to be made between straight economic objectives and goals which could broadly be termed social. The former are defined in terms of maximising the fund's income to provide the highest pension levels possible, the latter usually exemplified by reference to suggestions for employment-creating investment. Where such a trade-off was perceived, a variety of positions was possible. 'Social' investment might be regretfully rejected as impossible, or allowed only if it did not impinge on the economic objective. Others held that social objectives could not be ignored, but felt trapped by the system in view of their legal – and moral – obligations to their members. Since on this view attention to social objectives entailed a lower economic return, external action was necessary: 'There should be full accountability in investment. But it's not fair to take pension funds and penalise them. The government should act as financial intermediary.' In other words, a shift in the criteria and techniques used for assessing investment is necessary, but can only be achieved at some cost to the fund's traditional goals in a zero-sum game.

Running counter is the view that members' interests can *only* be properly secured if a broader approach is taken to investment policy (box 5(b)). Because of the growth of the funds they have a new responsibility to expand their objectives; the key point is that this new responsibility is not in conflict with the traditional ones but is in fact a necessary extension of them. The game is positive sum. The essence of the argument was bluntly expressed by an investment manager as follows:

The definition of members' interests in clearly being widened, in the sense that if the economy is not there then ICI shares (i.e. the typical investment outlets) are not likely to do well. The definition is not being tested in the law courts, but there is a growing awareness amongst fund managers that the economy needs to function if there are going to be tins of sardines or whatever it is that pensioners eat.

The broadening of responsibilities was similarly noted by the President of the Institute of Actuaries in his presidential address in 1982. Noting that 'some part of the flow of funds from pension schemes is not financing real investment, either directly or indirectly, but is at best recycling past borrowings and at worst financing current consumption', he added:

If there continues to be inadequate real investment, the time may come when the scale of occupational pension promises will have to be cut back. In the meantime we shall probably – and unfairly – allow unemployment and other changes in the structure of the workforce, aided by inflation, to alleviate the problem of eroding the pension rights of those affected. (Lyon, 1983, pp. 9, 10)

These remarks were made before the *Mineworkers' Pension Scheme* case which has brought the issue into the law courts with consequences that are at present hard to foresee. Until this case there had been very little legal action over the investment behaviour of the pension fund trustees. In *Evans v London Co-op* the Co-op was sued by a retired milkman for borrowing from the fund at a rate of interest lower than market rates; the judge found that trustees are allowed to take into account the interests of the members of the scheme qua employees, and not solely as future pensioners. But the *Mineworkers'* case put the issue in a much broader, and overtly political, context.

The case (*In re Mineworkers' Pension Scheme Trusts Cowan and Others v Scargill and Others*, to give it its legal adornment) was brought by the five trustees of the scheme appointed by the National Coal Board (NCB) against the five trustees appointed by the National Union of Mineworkers (NUM). The latter had refused to approve any investment plan which included investment abroad (in land or industry) or investment in sources of energy which might compete with coal. They were thus arguing for a narrowing of the spread of investments, on the grounds that this would be to the benefit of the mineworkers in two ways. Restricting investment to the UK would help the national economy, in whose reinvigoration both the NCB and the fund itself would share; and withholding investment from competing energy sources would directly improve the position of the coal industry and therefore of the miners, economically and in their employment prospects.

The judge, Sir Robert Megarry, found that the likelihood of such a policy by the Mineworkers' Scheme significantly affecting either the economy or its competitors was remote. On the former, even a fund as large as the Mineworkers' (£5 billion) could have little effect on its own. Commentators also pointed out that other investors would be likely to fill any holes left by the withdrawal of the fund's investments in oil or other energy sources.

Arguably the NUM were not particularly shrewd in their choice of grounds on which to fight the case. For example they might have argued at a more general level about the impact of pension funds as a whole on the economy and the need for a redefinition of trustee obligations. And the fact that they openly declared themselves bound by a resolution of the NUM conference made them more vulnerable, since trustees are not supposed to acknowledge such links. Whatever the technicalities of the case there are at least two points which it has raised and which are likely to be more widely discussed. The first is the notion of risk and the second is the nature of beneficiary interests. How *broadly* are these to be interpreted, and over what *timescale*? Is only the immediate (= annual?) financial return to be assessed, or should the trustees be able to have regard to other aspects of their members' lives, and be obliged to try to look rather further into the future than the average market analyst? To ask these questions is not to suggest that there are easy answers, a ready-made alternative to current financial orthodoxy; it is simply to suggest a possible redefinition of the parameters of the debate.[5]

The relevant point here is that although the judge found against the

NUM's attempt to alter the basis of the fund's investment policy, his judgement actually increased the flexibility of the notion of the 'beneficiary's interest'. He noted sagely that 'benefit' was a word with a very wide meaning. There might be circumstances in which action to the financial disadvantage of the beneficiary could yet be to his overall benefit, and he gave the example of adults with strict views on moral or social matters who might be deemed to benefit from not investing in areas such as tobacco or amusements, even though it demonstrably cost them something in terms of financial return. This is a far cry from allowing trustees to bring into their deliberations considerations about the best way of reinvigorating the national economy but it certainly does not shut the door on questions about how the interests of the members might take different forms at different levels of analysis on different timescales.

2. Personal constraints
There is obviously a very wide range of issues generated both by legal considerations and by technical disagreements, at different economic levels, over the policies to be pursued by the funds. Where experts are so much at variance, how can lay trustees be expected to reach their own conclusions on the best way of discharging their obligations? I turn now to consider constraints of a more personal nature: the kinds of experience and expertise possessed by member trustees, the advice sources available to them and the training provided for them. Although each of these is important, the conclusion should not be drawn that participation will only have a significant impact when member trustees attain a high level of technical competence. There is, certainly, disagreement over what levels of competence are required and in which areas, but it is not the trustee's responsibility to perform as stockbroker, economic analyst, actuary or any other professional role. We should avoid a simple polarisation of views on the relationship between trustees and advisers: either upholding the complete autonomy of the professionals, or seeing the relationship as one where the former issue instructions and the latter simply execute them. The first position is an advocacy of unaccountable passivity, the second a recipe for confusion. The question is rather what skills trustees need in order to be able to discharge their functions properly, including the establishment of an effective working relationship with their advisers.

Social and technical expertise
Decision-making is not an overt, mechanical process. It is shaped by a mass of informal and implicit procedures, whose rationale is sometimes only loosely rooted in grounds of technical efficiency. New participants enter an environment which may be very foreign to them. This is true of

almost any organisation: political parties and old people's clubs, as well as boards of directors. A clear instance of this, particularly relevant for our purposes since it dealt with participation at similar strategic decision-making levels, was the British Steel Corporation's initiatives with worker directors:

> Even if a worker had been appointed to the board who was likely to behave deviantly within the boardroom context, there were a number of other social processes at work, which we can label 'socialisation'...On the one hand the directors expected their new colleagues to accept conventions of boardroom behaviour and the overall goals of the board which they took for granted. In exchange they were willing to accept the worker directors as *bona fide* members and to listen to them as people who reflected a valid and reliable shop-floor perspective. (Brannen *et al.*, 1976, p. 235)

Member trustees often find themselves in circumstances which are even less familiar than those encountered by their worker-director counterparts. Board meetings are normally held at the company's headquarters, but they may also take place at the offices of the advisers, where the physical environment bears little resemblance to that of the run-of-the-mill office or factory: panelled walls, period furnishing and other accoutrements of flourishing financial institutions. On top of the different physical environment comes a different style of discourse, removed from the conventions of negotiation. The vocabulary is different, with talk of long-dated stock, venture capital and diversification of risk. This can lead to embarrassment, or to nervous quiescence; one trustee described his initial experience of investment committee meetings: 'At the start you pick out what you think are the failures, and make a mug of yourself. I was very lucky in that I was teamed up with the most experienced trustees. [But] f or about two years I never opened my mouth.' Friction can occur when there is a clash of conventions. The most extreme example of this was the fate of a member trustee who refused to switch from an orthodox bargaining mode of behaviour, as described by a fellow-trustee:

> There was a trustee director who was got rid of, not because of what he did at board meetings, but that let them know. He used to turn up wearing cowboy boots, four gold rings on one hand, you know the sort of thing. Also he wouldn't come to lunch with the rest of us, but strolled in on his own. Not long after he was fired, something to do with a strike in Birmingham.

To identify the social and technical conventions of boardroom practice as a constraint on the effectiveness of participants is not to imply that they are all artificial or repressive. Several trustees described how they had gradually learnt to develop their own ways of contributing to the discussions, recognising that pensions decision-making has its own specific character. There may be a residual sense of unease about the consensual nature of the process, especially for those brought up in a tradition of zero-sum game bargaining; on the other hand participation in any sort of joint decision-making, even orthodox negotiations, commonly entails at least provisional acceptance of rules and outcomes which are only partly satisfactory. Nevertheless, participation in pension fund management is a potentially significant form of economic democracy precisely because it entails decisions about the use of capital outside the organisation itself, and for this reason it takes participants into particularly unfamiliar areas and roles.

The main quality judged to be the essential attribute of the effective trustee was distinctly non-technical. It was most commonly defined in terms of the personal characteristic of common sense, and this is in accord with the legal notion of the 'prudent man'. Even this plain term can be given very varying degrees of robustness in its interpretation. One manager equated common sense with confidence in the pensions professionals, which the ideal trustee would exhibit in its fullest degree by accepting all the advice he was given. In other cases common sense was precisely the ability to know when simply to accept advice and when to ask pertinent questions.

As for specific areas of knowledge the most obvious issue is the degree of financial expertise required. Here there was a broad consensus, setting it at about the level of 'awareness that can be derived from fairly regular reading of the *Financial Times*'. This may sound rather arbitrary, but it certainly seemed to be widely regarded as a satisfactory compromise between total ignorance and formal qualifications. Yet it should perhaps be seen as a base level rather than a target; finance was quite clearly the area where training was felt to be most needed.

Not surprisingly, finance was also an area where company and member trustees were seen to diverge in their competence. At least some of the company trustees will have been appointed precisely because they have some financial responsibilities within the company. More generally, those occupying managerial posts can be expected to be at least acquainted with financial practices and terminology. Yet their professionalism in the area should not be exaggerated; as one manager remarked with some asperity 'sometimes management trustees assume they know things that they don't', and a finance director pointed out that it is a matter of degree: 'It is preferable [for member trustees] to have a knowledge of finance and of investment, but you can't expect union members to know it all and even I as a finance director don't have detailed expertise.'

One trustee put the question of expertise into perspective as follows:

> I felt at a loss until I read the merchant banker's report for the quarterly meeting: after the technical analysis comes a political analysis which is often faulty – they've only lifted it from the *Financial Times* or from City talk, and a national union official is usually equally capable of judging.

But such rapid acquisition of confidence is not universal. It is worth also citing the observation of one leading actuary: 'Although I would not wish to suggest that there is no such thing as investment expertise, I think that it is not so extensive as some investment managers might like their clients to believe, and we are having a lot of difficulty locating it' (Hager, 1982). On the other hand, member trustees may bring their own forms of expertise. A certain symmetry or complementarity is perceived between them and the other members of the board. 'Member trustees know a lot about pensions administration, which company trustees don't; it's vice versa about finance. And both have a lot to learn about the system as a whole – actuarial practice and so on.' On occasion this may take the form of raising issues which the professionals take for granted and have not paused to consider. This can be done in greater or less degrees of innocence. 'Asking a silly question can sometimes embarrass them [the advisers]. "Out of the mouths of babes..."' But one should not underestimate the confidence required to risk appearing foolish – and the even greater confidence required to take such a risk twice.[6]

The role of the actuary illustrates the ambiguities of expertise, though I cannot hope to lift the veil very far. The actuary has an important influence on fund strategy, for he defines the liabilities of the funds, and therefore the targets which are to be set for investment and contribution levels in order to meet these liabilities. There are three basic assumptions involved: the rate of return to the fund; the level of wage increases (and therefore of pensions, given that pensions are calculated in proportion to wages); and additional pension increases. This last often does not figure in the actuary's report; companies discourage it as it may encourage expectations. The key factor is the change in the *relationship* between the first two figures: not their absolute levels, but the gap between them. As long as this stays constant, there are no implications for the fund's solvency.[7] Because the company's contributions are dependent to a large degree on the view the actuary takes, it is not surprising that there is regularly an exchange of views between them. A partner in a senior firm of actuaries puts it:

> An actuary reporting to the trustees often discusses a draft of his report with the finance director of the company. The company's

contributions are invariably affected by the actuary's report, whether the actuary is appointed by the company or the trustees. (James, 1983)

There are two points here of interest. The first is whether the actuary's deliberations are also conveyed to the trustees, especially the reasons for any changes he may have made in his valuations. The second, especially relevant to our current concern with expertise, is the apparent malleability of the assumptions – not of the calculations which follow, but of the assumptions on which these sophisticated calculations are based. A legal judgement posed the issue as follows:

An actuary must employ expertise of great refinement which involves assessing the weight to be given to many and various contingencies and near imponderables. Some of these, such as mortality tables, may depend on statistical data and may be susceptible of more or less demonstrable validation. Others must necessarily be largely a matter of personal judgement. There is considerable scope for justifiable differences of opinion among actuaries, and as the actuary's function is essentially one of estimation, one actuary may very possibly reach a conclusion in a particular case which varies, perhaps widely, from the conclusion of another actuary on the same facts. (Quoted in Ellison, 1979, p. 335)[8]

Hannah (1986) records how discomfited the profession was by the uncertainties of the 1960s and 1970s. Sophisticated assumptions and calculations do have to be made; the question is how visible the processes are.

There are unquestionably types of expertise which the member trustee cannot expect to grasp in their entirety, but which are essential to any kind of efficient management. On the other hand there are also types whose justification is less inherently clear, and on which member trustees have little purchase. This may be a matter of deliberate managerial strategy, but is just as likely to be a matter of convention and routine. The key question is the extent to which the trustees can reasonably be considered to be discharging their formal obligations if they do not have access to the vaults of professional knowledge.

Finally, it is worth distinguishing between individual and collective expertise. A single trustee is not expected to possess all the qualities which the board as a corporate entity could embody. Arguably this distinction has emerged as a result of the influx of trustees from different social and occupational backgrounds. For all the emphasis on the unitary nature of trustee boards there is an implicit recognition that trustees will diverge in their attitudes and priorities. In order to preserve the spirit of cohesion, management may choose to stress the complementarity of qualities, with member trustees expected to specialise in personnel matters. The same phenomenon was observed in the Post Office's experiment with union representatives on the board:

> The priorities of the union nominees can be compared with those of the full-time members ... [Full-time members] focussed upon financial aspects and external relations with the state, suppliers and the consumer. 25% of their contributions (and 5% of the union nominees) focussed upon financial considerations and 29% (15% of the union nominees) upon external relations. 30% of full-time members' contributions concerned industrial relations and worker or union interests and attitudes, while proportionately twice as many of the union nominees' did so. (Batstone *et al.*, 1983, p. 81)

There is often a similar implicit division of labour, and expertise, within trustee boards.

Training and advice

The most obvious remedy for lack of expertise is to provide training. For industrial democracy in general, there are a number of questions relating to the content and style of the education, and to its control (Schuller, 1985, Chapter 9). In the case of member trustees it is the quantitative paucity of training which is most immediately apparent. Table 6.6 shows how minimal is the amount of training received.

Table 6.6: Training received by member trustees (member trustee survey)

Days	Number of recipients	
	Before becoming trustees	After becoming trustees
None	85	59
1 day	14	10
2–4 days	26	28
5 days	17	17
6–9 days	5	16
10 days	5	19
Over 10 days	2	9
No reply	18	14
	172	172

One-quarter of the trustees in the survey had received no training at all, either prior to assuming office or in the course of it. Including these, almost exactly half (49 per cent) had had no training beforehand, and one-third received only preparatory training and nothing subsequently. Even when some training is provided, it is generally scanty. The most common single amount was five days for preparatory and ten days for in-service training; but for the former over half and for the latter over one-third had three days or less.

Who provides the training? To repeat, the member trustee survey was conducted through trade unions, and the results therefore certainly overstate the level of union-provided training compared with the general population of trustees. The responses indicated that unions were marginally the biggest single source of training, in 68 cases compared with 59 instances of employer provision. Union courses tend to be longer than those of the employers, fitting in with the more widely established five-day and ten-day patterns of conventional shop steward courses. On the whole, however, there is no strong tradition of union training, and trustees are most likely to receive training which is laid on by the employer. In most cases it inevitably reflects the current orthodoxies – a half-day tour round the Stock Exchange being a classic example.

If the impact of member trustees is in itself difficult to identify in any specific fashion, it is not likely that the effects of training will show up very clearly.[9] Almost all of the trustees who had received training said they found it useful or very useful. They also felt that additional training would help them to perform their duties more effectively; whether this is to be taken as a comment on the inadequacy of existing provision or an appreciation of the value of the additional training is a matter of interpretation. Predictably there was a particularly high level of demand for more financial matters, either generally (39 per cent of those who indicated a preference) or specifically in relation to investment issues.

Table 6.7: Most common source of advice for member trustees (member trustee survey)

Source	Number
Union workplace negotiator	6
Full-time official	8
Union pensions officer	24
Employer pensions department	97
Employer industrial relations department	12
Independent pensions adviser	15
No reply	10
	172

Formal training is only one means by which a representative acquires expertise, and in the case of member trustees it is a very minor means. We have already pointed, for example, to the socialising influences which bear on a trustee as soon as he enters the boardroom. Alongside participation in organised courses or seminars comes the source of advice or information to whom the trustee most often has recourse. Table 6.7 shows that by far the most common source of information is the employer's pension department. This is natural, given the concentration identified earlier on a personnel role. Member trustees are primarily concerned with discretionary powers and information, and the pensions department is the most obvious source from which they may seek details on individual cases and guidance on rules and their implementation. The picture might change if there was a shift in the trustee's activity focus to the more strategic issues. But in any case there is no evident alternative source of information. Although more unions are building up a certain expertise on pensions, their priority is to help negotiators deal with questions of benefits and contributions, and they are rarely equipped to cater for the very different needs of trustees. Even if they were flush with resources it is far from clear precisely what role they should play, since the trustee is a different kind of animal to most of the representatives they service.

There were very few reports of trustees being prevented from getting information which they actively sought, though one reported plaintively that he kept asking in vain for a definition of 'surplus'. Four-fifths of the trustees surveyed said they had never been unable to obtain information on a particular issue – where there were difficulties it was usually over investment details. Here again there is at least the possibility that disclosure of information to trustees might be more of an issue if they were clearer about what they needed to know to be more effective. All that can be reported on that score is a mild degree of self-censorship, with some trustees not bothering to request information because they were sure it would not be forthcoming.

Conclusion

This chapter has drawn on survey and case study evidence to explore the pattern of contributions which member trustees make to pensions decision-making and the influence which those contributions are judged to have had. The pattern of contributions was found to divide along the cleavage identified at the beginning of the book, with the member trustees' contributions concentrating on personnel issues as distinct from issues of strategic capital control. Attention was then focussed on this latter area, given the context of economic democracy in which participation in pension fund management had been set, and a number of factors identified which could be seen as constraints on the impact of participation. These ranged from structural features to do with the constitution of the occupational pension scheme system itself to more personal characteristics such as expertise and training.

Two brief points may be made in conclusion. The first is to stress the limitations of the data, without being too apologetic. Bringing together survey and case study material gives both depth and breadth to a degree, but I have not tried to force them into an artificially seamless whole. The results are more suggestive of future lines to be explored for a fuller understanding rather than providing a definitive account.

The second is to underline the sense of potential expressed. Several respondents, from management and union, expressed agreeable surprise at the abilities revealed by member trustees – not always phrased in the patronising fashion that this might suggest. For others the impact of participation lay more in the future. Very rarely was there a feeling that any sort of ceiling had been reached in the degree of member trustee effectiveness. In judging the impact of this type of participation, a very particular temporal perspective is required. The growth of the funds has been explosive, but the pace of pensions decision-making is more leisurely than most corporate processes, the accumulation of *savoir faire* more protracted. Most member trustees are neophytes; even several years in office may not mean that they have attended more than a handful of meetings where they have caught the threads firmly. Who knows what the learning curve will be?

Notes

1. The provision of such information can be a source of acrimony. Minns describes the Annual General Meeting of the Lucas pension fund. There had been friction between the company and the unions over access to information, and a scrimmage developed around the single copy of the fund's investment portfolio that was made available (1980, p. 137).
2. The pattern is broadly confirmed by the BIM survey referred to earlier.
3. A 1984 circular from the Institute of Actuaries contains the following advice:

   In the light of recommendations made by the Occupational Pensions Board and of proposals by the accountancy bodies, the practice of supplying annual reports by trustees to scheme members is likely to grow. To the extent that such reports contain information from actuaries on the financial position of a scheme, it is important that such information should be expressed in terms which can be understood by members. (Institute of Actuaries, 1984)

4. This partly reflects the fact that the case studies mostly had developed internal management structures; external advisers figured more strongly in response to a similar question in the member trustee survey, in which there was a lower proportion of large organisations.
5. See Nobles (1985) for a more detailed discussion of the legal issues involved. See also the comment of Ralph Quartano, head of the investment team managing £10 billion of assets owned by the Post Office and British Telecom pension funds: 'I know how to assess the riskiness of a share by measuring the volatility of its price compared with the market as a whole. What I do not understand is risk as it applies to a 40-year pension scheme. I wish I could crack that' (*Observer*, 28 April 1985).
6. Member trustees may in future be helped by the TUC guide (1984) which provides them with a series of questions on issues such as performance measurement,

accounting procedures and actuarial practice, but this was published after the fieldwork for the research was concluded.

7. Thus if at one valuation the rate of return is assumed to be 9 per cent and the rate of wage increase 7 per cent, what is important at the next valuation (normally three years later) is that the gap between the two should remain at 2 per cent; it may be alarming for other reasons if the figures rocket up to 17 per cent and 15 per cent respectively but in principle it does not affect the fund's liabilities. If, on the other hand, the rate of return drops to 7 per cent but the projected rate of wage increases goes down only to 6 per cent, the solvency of the fund is affected, and the actuary may feel obliged to recommend a rise in the level of contributions.

8. One critic of professional mystique is highly caustic:

> Whether it is because few people know who or what an actuary is, whether it is the mathematical expertise, or whether it is the magical connotations of 'life-tables', in terms of professional mystique actuaries leave doctors and lawyers far behind. Yet when one examines the heroism of their assumptions and the inconsistency, often negativity, of the *real* returns on pension fund investments, their analysis can look very flimsy indeed. (Piachaud, 1983, p. 279)

9. See Robertson (1981) for the difficulty of evaluating union training.

7 Strategic Participation and Social Contracts

> Pensions are unique because of the obligations involved, but it could well be that it [the experience of participation] would transfer across to corporate affairs. For example, our four member trustees are quite capable of being non-executive directors of company boards. (Pensions manager)

There is within the pensions fraternity a pride in their particular identity. Pension systems have their private vocabulary and mystique, and specific legal and administrative intricacies. For many managerial and employee representatives pensions are an area set apart from the daily turbulences of corporate business and industrial relations, with its own rules and style of decision-making. On the other hand, pensions are being pulled more into the mainstream of corporate affairs, both as a major item of occupational welfare and because of the capital sums involved, which impinge heavily on coporate assets and liabilities. The rise of participation in pensions may therefore have wider implications. How far is pensions participation *sui generis* and how far does it mesh into the broader pattern of democracy at work?

Once again I shall concentrate on the trustee level. It is not the only mode of participation, but I have dealt quite extensively with the relation between pensions bargaining and other forms of negotiation in Chapter 3, and it would be impossible to draw together all the diverse forms of participation and consultation. Moreover, it is at the level of the trustee board that the issue of capital control emerges to establish the link between economic and industrial democracy. The natural comparison is, then, between member trustees and worker directors, since both operate at the strategic level of decision-making, though many of the parallels and contrasts hold more generally for the field of participation and are not confined to the boardroom. The parallels may be explored under the broad headings of the rationale for participation, its objectives and its legitimation.

Take first the question of *rationale* for participation, which can be looked at in terms of *rights* and of *functions*. The most obvious basis for participation in pensions decision-making as a matter of right is the acceptance of the deferred pay concept. Allowing for the argument that it is ultimately the employer's responsibility to ensure that pensions are paid and the employer's right to wind up the scheme, the notion that it is 'their money' constitutes the basis of the members' right to representation in how the money is managed.[1] On one view, participation in the management of the pension fund is therefore fundamentally different from participation in the management of the company itself because the fund belongs to the members whereas the company belongs to its shareholders. The legal and constitutional circumstances are indeed different, but the question of rights suggests two parallels.

First, part of the rationale behind many of the moves towards greater industrial democracy is that working people invest a good part of their lives in the firm or firms in which they are employed, and this should endow them with the right to something more than a weekly or monthly wage. The EEC Green Paper on employee participation and company structure referred to the 'democratic imperative', which it interpreted as follows: 'Those who will be substantially affected by decisions made by social and political institutions *must* be involved in the making of those decisions' (1975, p. 9, my stress). The force of the obligation in the face of current economic crises is open to question; but it formed a major plank in the Bullock Committee's rationale for worker directors. It seemed to the Committee, 'as it did to most witnesses that to regard the company as solely the property of the shareholders is to be out of touch with the reality of the present day company as a complex social and economic entity' (1977, p. 141).[2] The Committee's repeated reference to the need for a balance between the interests of employees and shareholders is clearly incompatible with the view that the investment of capital in an enterprise brings with it rights that have an absolute priority over the claims of those who invest their labour. This is a significant ideological shift, and was not fundamentally challenged by the Minority Report issued by the Committee members who dissented from the main report's chief proposals. Section 46 of the 1980 Companies Act imposes on directors the duty of having regard to the interest of employees as well as shareholders. This may not so far have had much actual effect, but it is a further reflection of movement in the social perceptions of the basis on which the right to strategic decision-making is exercised.

This is nowhere near as concrete a basis for participation as the shift from gratuity to deferred pay in the case of pension funds. That shift is significant, both conceptually and (as it turns out) in terms of the capital sums involved, and it clearly demonstrates that the boundaries of ownership rights are not immovably fixed. Yet whilst the links between rights and representation are less clear in the case of general corporate policy than in the specific case of pensions, we are in both cases talking about rights to influence decisions over the use as well as the distribution of surplus created, deriving from workers' investment of their labour in the organisation. How revenues are to be accumulated, invested or distributed is not only an item on the negotiating agenda of individual organisations but the object of a much wider political concern over the creation and control of wealth.[3]

Secondly, the notion that rights, however they are derived, yield clearcut and overriding powers is patently inadequate as a guide to behaviour. Obligations, the obverse of rights, are also entailed. Even if employees achieve board level representation in recognition of their contribution to the firm's economic activity, neither they nor their shareholder counterparts have unfettered freedom. There are constraints on both common owners and private capitalists, some of a strictly legal nature and others reflecting broader social and economic factors. Ideologically it is increasingly difficult to defend the right of owners of capital, whether individuals or institutions, to use that capital as they see fit without regard to its impact on the rest of society. There are, of course, plenty of examples where this does occur, sometimes with calamitous effects on employees, on the physical environment or on communities, but the mere fact of ownership cannot justify indifference to the consequences of capital allocation. In the case of pension funds there is a nascent recognition that the size of the funds collectively places the issue of responsible behaviour by their masters in a new light. This is a very far cry from a wholesale change in the framework of accountability within which economic institutions operate, but it hints at the shifting relationships between rights and obligations, to which participation gives a further twist.

In short, the history of pensions is enough to demonstrate how ideas of rights change over time. In this case, they have evolved from the gratuity notion where the employer retains unilateral control to a much more complex form of entitlement. The rights are not yet firmly established, and the obligations which accompany those rights far from clear. But pensions may be part of broader changes in public perceptions of property rights, leading to fresh alignment of power and responsibility in decision-making.[4]

The second form of rationale suggests that participation is functionally useful for the efficiency of the organisation. This was discussed in Chapters 4 and 6 in relation to member trustees; the broad consensus shown by the case study respondents on the positive value of participation was based on the usefulness of member trustees as legitimators of the system and as channels of information. In other words, even if there was no substance to the claim for representation on the basis of right it would still make sense to include member trustees on the ground that it increases the efficiency of the scheme, defined in terms of the members' well-being. Similar arguments were put forward by the Bullock Committee in relation to worker directors. They referred to the

TUC's view that industrial democracy involving a board with parity employee and shareholder representation could provide a new legitimacy for the exercise of the management function and commented:

> Given the increasing tendency...for employees to question more traditional bases of managerial authority, this could be a key factor in making possible the fruitful co-operation between management and labour needed to tackle and overcome our current industrial problems. (1977, Chapter 4, paragraph 8)

Such arguments are common to many of the cases put forward for an extension of participation generally, in the political as well as the industrial sphere. Neglect of the knowledge and energies of the broad population is a common criticism levelled against non-democratic regimes and has a good deal of intuitive appeal, though hard-nosed empirical evidence is difficult to supply. But the question of what is 'functional' requires some reflection, and points to an issue common in debates about worker directors but only beginning to emerge in the field of pensions. How far is a unitary view to prevail, which sees decision-making within organisations as the rational blending of common interests in what is essentially a positive sum game? Does everyone benefit by greater employee representation, or does it pose a threat to the interests (material or ideological) of some of the parties? Alternatively, is it a means whereby management retains control, consciously or unconsciously incorporating employees into the existing system and sharing only as much power as is necessary to avoid having to concede more? If everyone shares a common interest in pensions, then this 'incorporation' argument has no validity, and the functionalist rationale is unproblematic. If, on the other hand, there are underlying distributive issues at stake so that one party's gain means another's loss, there is at least a case for seeing participation as a strategy, deliberate or not, for preserving the current distribution pattern. The question of 'functional for whom?' then becomes particularly relevant.

At trustee level pensions decision-making is seen very generally as a consensual affair. In contrast to the historical origins of profit-sharing schemes, the introduction by management of participation has not been a direct response to labour unrest or overt challenges to managerial legitimacy. But this comfortably unitary perspective may not continue to prevail. In the first place, the tendency for pensions to become a negotiable item outside the trustee board generates waves which nudge, however gently, against the trustee boat. The emergence of fund surpluses and the question of how they are to be distributed will add choppiness to the waves. Secondly, there are strains within pension schemes over the relative positions of different groups of members –

most obviously, but not exclusively, stayers against early leavers. Thirdly, as occupational pensions figure more prominently as an item in overall corporate costs, the potential for friction between the rival claims of members and non-members (notably part-timers, and therefore women) becomes more pronounced. Fourthly, on a broader canvas, the extent of fiscal privilege (the tax exemption allowed to pension fund contributions and income and to lump-sum payments) has attracted political attention both from governments interested in increasing their revenues and more generally from those concerned with fiscal equity. There are, therefore, at least four lines of possible tension and although the introduction of member representation probably does in the short run strengthen the legitimacy of the schemes it provides no guarantee against the emergence of strains which have so far been largely latent. Against this background member trustees may, as they accumulate experience, begin to assert themselves on one side or the other of these dividing lines. The form this muscle-flexing will take is by no means clear; should trustees move away from their passive role the impact on the distribution of benefits and the allocation of capital is not easy to predict. The essential point here is that the functional rationale for participation cannot be made to depend directly on a wholly unitary model of pensions decision-making, with member trustees simply feeding in extra informational input to the board's deliberations.

The position of worker directors looks rather different in relation to functionality. There is a narrower base of experience on which to draw as evidence for their contribution to decision-making, as well as a lower degree of consensus on the right of representation. There are fewer managers willing to testify to the benefits of representation at this level, and the ideological debate about its legitimacy and effect has been far sharper. In particular, it has been argued that worker directors cannot do what the Companies Act suggests that all directors should do: look after the interests of employees as well as those of the company. In other words, they cannot maintain a dual allegiance to capital and to labour. On the other hand arguably the relationships between capital and labour are altering in ways which reduce the particular salience of the dual allegiance problem and lead to more complex notions of what is functional for whom. There is no unitary framework which allows worker directors to sit easily alongside their company counterparts. But whilst pensions decision-making shows more signs of strain and contestation, worker representation at board level may appear to both management and labour to involve less direct conflicts of role than it has done in the past, even if only to a very limited degree. If so, there is no absolute distinction to be made between the cases for member trustees and worker directors on the grounds that the former can operate functionally within a unitary framework whilst the latter cannot because boardroom decision-making always involves a peculiarly fundamental conflict of interest. I am not arguing that the frameworks within which pensions decision-making and corporate decision-making occur are straightforwardly converging, simply that both are changing in a way that makes the distinction in principle less absolute.

This in turn poses the question of the *objectives* of participation. The functionalist line of argument assumes that there is no conflict between the democratisation of decision-making and the quality of the organisation's performance. Opponents of this line tend to argue that the complexity of modern organisations or the nature of the capitalist system makes significant democracy impossible. One consequence of the debate being polarised in this way is that the difference between means and ends is obscured. It is perfectly possible that a greater measure of democracy may be based on good ethical grounds and yet impair the organisation's performance, however that is measured. Where this objection is made, it is usually by those whose interests are satisfactorily served by existing arrangements. So the idea of worker directors is rejected because it would reduce economic efficiency, as well as managerial control. In the case of pension scheme management, positive participation in investment policy may be seen as a threat to investment performance, as well as to the company's grip on the allocation of assets. On the other hand the case for greater democracy often leaves unstated the expected impact on performance, the implicit assumption being that the outcome will be recognisably of benefit to those who have newly gained representation. There are two points to be made in this connection.

The first is that there is no necessary link between democracy and efficiency, at least in the short run. It may well be that there is something of a trade-off to be made in immediate material terms. The prime disadvantage of participation cited by case study respondents was that it took time, and time is money. The process of decision-making may become more complicated and prolonged. This was generally reckoned to be a price worth paying, but it is a price nevertheless. Other costs may be involved, for example where the organisation operates in a market sector which requires snap decisions.

One should not assume, however, that the notion of 'efficiency' remains constant, unaffected by democratisation. In greater or lesser ways the objectives of the organisation may be altered and the criteria for assessing its performance modified. In the case of pension fund management it might be argued in very broad terms that pensioners are not best served by receiving a marginally higher benefit if they have to live in environments blighted by economic decay and mass unemployment; in the case of general corporate policy that a single-minded focus on economic criteria is not desirable even though it rewards employees with higher wages, if it involves physical pollution, unethical behaviour or any of the other characteristics of unrestrained profit-seeking. Yet there is no guarantee that greater participation will shift behaviour in a particular direction. 'Corporate egotism' for example – looking after one's own (collective) interests at the expense of others – is just as possible in an organisation with member trustees or worker directors as one without them. And within the organisation itself the problems of reconciling conflicting objectives will not necessarily diminish because of greater participation.

The second point is closely related. Who is to be represented, and by whom (assuming that the democratic form is at least to a degree representative and does not involve direct participation by all those concerned)? Only half of the working population are covered by occupational pension schemes. They are heavily subsidised by the other half, who contribute through their economic activity to the public revenues which give fiscal support to the schemes. More specifically, these 11 million members work in organisations which employ 16 million people. There are therefore about five million people who work alongside pension scheme members and contribute to the same organisation's economic performance but are excluded from membership of the pension scheme as a share in the fruits of that performance. What are their rights and expectations, and how well will they be safeguarded by a representative system based on membership of the scheme? Given the importance of pensions as an item of corporate costs, the greater the amount devoted to pensions the less there is potentially available for distribution elsewhere, whether this be directly in the form of wages, in other benefits or in improving the organisation's economic position through new investment.

One can go a step further. Within the scheme itself, will participation ensure equitable behaviour? Very few schemes have pensioners represented on the trustee boards, partly because of the organisational problems involved in establishing a system which would allow a pensioner to be selected in representative fashion. The more powerful the representatives of members who are current employees, the more they might act to weight the system in favour of themselves, at the expense of the unrepresented. This may sound unduly cynical and it is not intended at all as a description of current behaviour. But it illustrates the potential polarisation inherent in representative systems from which certain groups are excluded.[5]

The same is true of participation more generally, though it is more difficult to identify clearly broad segments of the population. Participation may be the preserve of a certain segment of the workforce, so that the intrinsic good of participating and the benefits which flow from it are not equitably distributed. There will be a constant tension between the incentive to safeguard and promote the interests of the core labour force and the idea that there might be responsibilities to a broader population. Co-operatives have very few opponents in principle, but one theoretical line of criticism is that existing members of co-ops will be reluctant to expand the business and bring in new co-operators because it could materially damage their own interests (Meade, 1982). In a rather different context, evidence from West Germany suggests that their renowned system of works councils tends to favour male skilled Germans at the expense of women, the unskilled and migrant labour (Batstone, 1976). The same may be true of worker directors, for there is no inherent reason why they should consider themselves obliged to pursue equity as a goal, or any of the other objectives which are commonly bracketed with greater democracy. Constitutional reform alone is not enough to achieve the goals aspired to by the more optimistic proponents of democratisation. Discussion of the value of participation cannot be confined to the nature of its formal structures.

More broadly the upsurge in unemployment has accentuated the danger of polarisation between those in secure jobs and those who are without employment or who float uncomfortably around in the margins of the labour force. Once again, there is no single-dimensional polarity, as deep cleavages persist within those in employment relationships. But those who do have jobs may enjoy, in addition to a regular pay cheque and a degree of occupational welfare, a measure of influence over their own working environment (Schuller, 1984). Employee participation has little meaning for those who are not employees. In short, participation is not necessarily a socially bonding force. The issue which formed the nub of the historical opposition between syndicalism and guild socialism is still with us: however fully developed the internal democracy of a particular organisation, there remains the task of balancing its needs and desires with those of the broader population.

The *legitimacy* of representatives is linked to but distinct from the legitimacy they afford to the system, which I discussed earlier. One of the reasons for the demise of the Bullock proposals was their failure to win genuine widespread support even amongst those for whose benefit they were formulated. Covert bargaining secured the assent of many union leaders to the thrust of the proposals, but not necessarily that of their members; and in the population as a whole the unease caused by the summary assertion of the single channel principle (that the selection of worker directors should be carried out through union machinery) arguably outweighed the positive attraction of democratisation. As a consequence there was less broad-based support to draw on than there might have been in defence of the proposals against the sustained attack of their opponents.[6] Legitimacy derives from a number of factors and a single line of argument from the top, however cogent, is not usually sufficient to justify a universal formula. To be fair, the Report's proposals took account of this; but the manner of their own formulation excluded popular mobilisation.

In pension schemes the threat of legislation contributed to the spread of participation, but it was accompanied by a number of other factors (see Chapter 4). Predictably there was more hostility amongst managerial than employee representatives to the idea of compulsion on participation, but even amongst the former group it was not uncommon to find support, albeit reluctant, for legislation as a means of bringing laggards into line. So although genuine legitimacy cannot be achieved by the wave of a legislative wand, there is scope for imposing legal obligations where the ground has been properly prepared.

Legitimacy depends as much on the objectives which the representatives are seen to pursue as on the rationale which put them where they are. The legitimacy of a representative or set of representatives may be threatened not so much by the inherent quality or otherwise of the policies pursued as by the extent to which those represented see them as justified. The efforts of a member trustee or worker director to put through good policies may simply not be appreciated by those whom they were designed to help. The problem is most acute for strategic level participation because of the clash of temporal perspectives. It is far easier for members to give their support to decisions which bring immediate apparent gain than to those with a longer-term objective. This is not only a matter of deferring gratification, but of grasping the inherently greater complexities of longer-term decision-making. This applies generally, and certainly makes the legitimacy of worker directors more difficult to achieve. Member trustees at least have the advantage that pension schemes are universally acknowledged to be about providing for the future, so that a perspective of sorts is already established. The problem of justifying particular decisions on the basis of longer-term interests remains.

Accountability is a key component of legitimacy, and indeed is indissociable from democracy more generally. In a literal sense, it is to do with explaining and justifying what one has done, to people who have some degree of power to approve or reject the accounts rendered. In the case of pensions trustees this is obviously important given their essentially supervisory role yet it is evident that there is no consistency of practice, either in the detail of the accounts given or in the precision required. It may be that mounting pressure for better information will lead to more consistency. Meanwhile there are two general points to be made. First, there is the extent to which professional management is accountable to the trustees themselves. We have already given the specific illustration of the actuary who consults with the employer rather than the trustees. At the level of information, it is at least questionable whether many trustees themselves receive a clear enough picture to be able in turn to present to their members their own accounts of how the assets are being managed.

Secondly there is the extent to which participation at the strategic level is complemented by participation at other levels establishing a firmer link between apex and base. In a sub-sample of scheme members in the Glasgow case studies over one-third of the members simply did not know whether or not there were representatives acting on their behalf in the scheme.[7] The explanation for differences in awareness was not to be found in the amount or quality of information provided, but in the degree to which participation extended to the periphery of the organisation (Hyman and Schuller, 1983). Thus a company might perfectly well pay great attention to its personal information system, but if decision-making bodies exist only on a central basis the odds are against members scattered round the country being aware that they are in principle participating.

The inference is perhaps an obvious one, but should be related to the discussion about means and ends. Effective participation may be judged in terms of the impact made by representatives at board level on decisions within the board. With their multiple functions and amateur status trustees may be preoccupied primarily with learning the ropes and preparing their contributions in order to make such an impact. But effective participation measured in these terms is not necessarily accompanied by any active assent to the representation from the shop floor. Even where member trustees have had a demonstrable influence on the dissemination of information this may not be recognised by the members concerned. In both cases – pensions and general participation – the quality and character of information provided by professionals to representatives on the board will always be an issue, as will the extent to which the latter are free, able and willing to pass it on down. And the nature of the structure which the strategic body tops off will always affect the character of the contract between representative and represented.

This has been a broad-brush attempt to sketch out some of the parallels between pensions participation and other forms of participation. Though the points apply generally to the theme of participation, the focus has been on board-level participation – in spite of the remark by one manager that 'the directors would have gone mad if they'd thought it had anything to do with worker directors'. Other parallels could have been explored, for example the uncertain nature of the competences required by representatives involved in strategic decision-making: who defines what is a 'good' worker director or member trustee, and how are they to acquire these qualities? The broad conclusion is similar to that on collective bargaining: pensions can to a degree – perhaps increasingly – be aligned with other areas of policy, but retain their own distinguishing features. There is, however, a significant difference between the balance of experience accumulated at the levels of the collective bargaining and of strategic decision-making. On bargaining, pensions are a relatively belated newcomer to a field where there is a wealth of experience stretching over many decades, on which pensions negotiators can draw. At the strategic level the position is to a degree reversed: participation on trustee boards is far more widespread than on company boards. Many of these member trustees have only been in office a short time and there is as yet little accumulated experience to draw on. Boards of trustees diverge markedly from company boards in ethos and rationale as well as subject-matter, so the experience is not directly transferable. Nevertheless, the experience of member trustees, properly absorbed, should yield much in the way of lessons for further participation in other fields.

Conclusion: Social Divisions and Social Contracts

At the most general level of analysis, the simple dichotomy between the buyers and sellers of labour power seems less and less adequate as a basis for exploring patterns of social division. Without entering into the whole issue of class and class structure, one can point to the growth of home ownership and the concomitant importance of housing tenure as a major, if not the major, dividing line in British society. The distribution of power and wealth remains very unequal, but if class theory is elaborated only with reference to ownership of the means of production it becomes overextended to the point of meaninglessness.[8] The growth of pension funds has further clouded the very notion of 'capitalism' in its traditional sense of an economy dominated by private ownership. They constitute, to a degree, the partial collectivisation of the economy through the trend away from individual ownership; they are, moreover, impeding its reprivatisation in the full sense of the term as assets sold off in the name of denationalisation and the revival of individual capitalism find their way rapidly back into institutional ownership. There is, of course, a major gap between this formal semi-collectivisation and practical measures of common accountability and control. But the trend has brought a large segment of the population into a dual role, as consumers and owners. Pension scheme members are the individual consumers, current and future, of the benefits which flow from the funds. They are also, with all the qualifications mentioned earlier, the collective owners of the assets. At present it is the former role which dominates: members are more concerned with their own benefit position than with their collective rights as owners of the capital, and their interest in investment issues is mostly confined to how the performance of their fund affects their future pension. Attitudes resemble those of participants in profit-sharing schemes, with interest confined to their individual financial position. Yet this does not in principle undermine their position as collective owners of accumulations of capital in which they have a stake and in whose direction they are entitled to participate.

I have already described how different interest groups may be constituted within single schemes, and the structural problems of combining collective interests above the level of the individual scheme. My summary point here is simply that the growth of scheme membership and assets, founded on substantial public subsidy, has given a new complexion to the relationship between ownership, the definition of interest groups and the pattern of social division. This rather sweeping statement can be illustrated by turning directly to the contracts implicit in the occupational pension system and picking up the themes of the opening chapter. The management of pension schemes can be seen in terms of three types of contract: between society and its older members; between the managers of capital and those affected by its disposition; and between the members of the schemes and the people who represent them. In each case it is a fair guess that the contract will shift towards a higher level of explicitness, away from the more covert, implicit or routine forms of relationship which currently characterise them. It is in the nature of such shifts that they will uncover more or less significant strains and tensions; less surely, that they will generate new approaches to the resolution of those tensions. At the same time the mutual compatibility of the separate contracts will come more into question.

On the one hand the occupational scheme system is founded on the principle that risks should be pooled and provision for old age made on a collective basis. If portable pensions are introduced this would mark a significant shift away from this principle, with individuals supposedly assuming a greater measure of personal responsibility for securing their own income at the end of their working lives. On the other hand, occupational pensions are far from being a comprehensive form of collective provision, and not only because they cover only half of the working population. Their existence, and the public subsidy which supports them, inevitably impinge on the ability of the state to provide for the pensioner population as a whole. This is in part because of the fiscal subsidy they receive. But it is also because of the way any occupation-based welfare system gives an added twist to the division between those with and those without stable employment. The social nature of the contract between different generations is severely circumscribed by the massive presence of the occupational system. Although the system may, as we saw in Chapter 1, facilitate the transition into retirement and give decent living standards to some pensioners, it is simply not designed to tackle general questions of the equitable distribution of benefits amongst the population as a whole.[9]

Nor is it designed to bring into balance the broader implications of the use of the capital involved with the specific obligation to supply benefits.

Efficient fund management is crucial for the economic health of the country and the well-being of pensioners. But the current pattern of asset concentration and distribution has little to do with logic or design. The problems involved will not be easily solved, either by decomposing the funds into individual portions or by wholesale amalgamation into a comprehensive state system. I make no judgement on whether it is desirable to aim for a greater or lesser degree of collectivisation than currently exists. The occupational system, emerging after years of struggle towards a political consensus, may now be so integral a part of the pensions scene and of the fabric of British capital that its restructuring is at least in the short term not feasible. The fact that it is in many ways flawed does not necessarily mean that it should be dismantled. But given the haphazard history of pensions, it is worth stressing the extent to which the funds have been drawn into an economic role which they were never intended to play. They are part of a vast nexus of financial institutions whose practices enmesh the contract between managers and members in a much broader system of capital control, as we saw in Chapter 5.

This in turn sets the context for the third type of contract, between representatives and members. What is the likely future shape of this contract? On the one hand there is already pressure for a clearer specification of trustee duties, which should help to define member trustees' relationship with scheme members as long as the issue is confined to the management of individual schemes. On the other hand, if the responsibilities of the trustees are interpreted more broadly, in the light of the funds' asset size and economic impact, then the relationship becomes less simple and direct. Even if the primary obligation remains to the particular scheme members, what is the balance to be between this primary obligation and broader secondary ones, such as the promotion of economic growth and stability on behalf of the population as a whole, future pensioners included? Who exactly are the trustees representing: the owners of the funds, the beneficiaries of the revenues or some or all of those affected by their allocation?

The issue as I have outlined it – the shifting relationship between ownership, interest definition and social division – goes far beyond occupational pension schemes. It involves the whole system of financial institutions glanced at in Chapter 5. But the trend towards more explicit forms of contract should, I suggest, give prominence to three very general and interrelated questions:

(1) Philosophically, what changes can we envisage in the definition of the rights and obligations of investors, especially the institutions?
(2) Technically, what changes do we need in the practices of management?

(3) Politically, what forms of accountability are to be envisaged which are both practical and adequate?

A quarter of a century ago, Richard Titmuss observed in his pamphlet on *'The Irresponsible Society:'* 'The last decade has witnessed something of an explosion in the accumulation of immense funds in the hands of private insurance companies and pension trusts.' He concluded: '...we do not know how this power is being used in terms of social welfare priorities or how far these massive investment funds are being or will be used to restore the outworn, mid-Victorian social capital of Britain' (1960, pp. 13, 15). We still do not know. Half a century earlier, Walter Bagehot introduced 'Lombard Street' in a passage that is relevant today:

> We cannot appeal, therefore, to experience to prove the safety of our system as it now is, for the present magnitude of that system is entirely new. Obviously a system may be fit to regulate a few millions and yet quite inadequate to cope with many millions. And this it *may* be with 'Lombard Street', so rapid has been its growth and so unprecedented its nature.
>
> I am by no means an alarmist. I believe that our system, though curious and peculiar, may be worked safely; but if we wish so to work it, we must study it. We must not think we have an easy task when we have a difficult task, or that we are living in a natural state when we are really living in an artificial state. Money will not manage itself, and Lombard Street has a great deal of money to manage. (1912, p. 20)

Notes

1. Most trust deeds specify the following order of precedence in the case of a scheme being wound up: current pensioners first, then deferred annuitants currently employed, then early leavers' deferred annuities and finally the return of any surplus to the employer.
2. On the level of legal technicality, an authoritative contribution to the debate over Bullock argued that 'the interests of the company' as contained in company law need not in every case involve the interests of the shareholders. (See Davies and Wedderburn, 1977)
3. In this context and in the light of the debate over trustee obligations, the remark of Andrew Carnegie at the turn of the century is worth quoting:

    > [The man of wealth] must consider all surplus revenues which come to him simply as trust funds, which he is called upon to administer, and strictly bound as a matter of duty to administer in a manner which, in his judgement, is best calculated to produce the most beneficial results for the community. (1900, p. 13)

    Carnegie of course will have had equally definite views on how 'surplus' is to be defined.
4. An ambitious and substantial discussion of this issue in relation to capital generally is to be found in Horvat (1982).
5. Hannah observes that it was only possible in the 'undeveloped democracy' of late

Strategic Participation and Social Contracts 153

Victorian Britain, where the poor were unlikely to have the vote and anyway lost it on entering the workhouse, that 'a generation enjoying comfortably improving real living standards refused to share them more than proportionately with the aged needy' (1986, Chapter 1, p. 8). It may be that the mature democracy of today is not so firm in its commitment to equitable distribution as this implies. But the more salient comparison may be with the degree of democratic participation in the management of old age: just as the elderly poor could be disregarded then because of their lack of political franchise, so they may now be treated as marginal because of their lack of an 'occupational franchise', that is the right to participate.

6   This is not to say that union-based schemes are necessarily illegitimate and command little popular assent. The West German system is *de facto* very largely union-based (Marsden, 1978). In the UK the Post Office experiment learnt the lesson from BSC's attempt to sever work directors from their union bases and built its system through union structures with no apparent damage to its credibility (Batstone *et al.*, 1983).
7   There were, in addition, a small number who positively but incorrectly affirmed that there was no representation.
8   Saunders, for example, has argued convincingly that private-home ownership generates 'consumption sector cleavages' that must be taken just as seriously as class alignments based on ownership in the production sector (1984).
9   See van Gunsteren and Rein (1985) for a discussion of the tension between public and private pension systems, and the effect on notions of solidarity.

Appendix: The Glasgow Research

Some readers will recall the chocolate-bar wrapper depicting a man at successive stages of life, ranging from 25 to 65. The first picture shows him smiling and carefree, with the caption: 'They tell me the job has no pension'; the last shows him with heavily furrowed brow, regretting that 'Without a pension I really don't know what I shall do.' My awareness of pensions as an issue began whilst preparing training materials for worker representatives as part of a project commissioned following the Bullock Report. I was casting about for a small, self-contained side-issue which could be used to illustrate some of the issues confronting representatives involved in new areas of decision-making, and pensions seemed to fit the bill. It was only gradually that I became aware of the size, the range and the complexity of the issues involved.

Eventually a submission to the Leverhulme Trust for research funding was successful. The project was carried out during 1982 and 1983 by myself and Jeff Hyman, with the help of Laurie Hunter, at Glasgow University's Centre for Research in Industrial Democracy and Participation. (It is worth adding, as a comment on the problems facing contract researchers today, that although we were able to write up a good proportion of the results in article form, there was no chance of writing a book together within the project's timeframe. This is no criticism of the Trust, whose support has been consistent and generous.) The original intention was to carry out a smallish postal survey, followed by about 20 case studies. In the event the research comprised five components:

(1) A detailed postal survey of *pensions managers*. A sample of 500 was drawn on a random 1-in-5 basis from a published register of pension funds. We received 146 responses, a response rate of just under 30 per cent. This may seem unacceptably low, but the great majority of the non-respondents were small schemes; these tend to be fully insured and therefore not to have trustees (see p. 68). Schemes with over 1000 members, by contrast, constitute only a small proportion of all schemes – about 2 per cent – but they cover about 70 per cent of the total membership. So there is a bias to larger schemes, but on the other hand these cover the bulk of scheme members. In the tables in Chapters 4 and 6, the figures from the pensions manager survey are

based on the overall total of 146. Where they present data on schemes with member trustees, the base total is 70. There are minor fluctuations in both these totals reflecting the occasional omitted reply to a particular question.

(2) *A parallel survey of member trustees.* These were identified and contacted with the co-operation of seven trade unions: APEX (Association of Professional, Executive, Clerical and Computer Staff), ASTMS (Association of Scientific, Technical and Managerial Staffs), BIFU (Banking, Insurance and Finance Union), EETPU (Electrical, Electronic, Telecommunications and Plumbing Union), GMWU (General and Municipal Workers Union – now GMBATU after its merger with the Boilermakers' union), TGWU (Transport and General Workers Union) and USDAW (Union of Shop, Distributive and Allied Workers). There is no general register of trustees from which we could have drawn a sample directly. Clearly, therefore, this sample is biased towards union-based representatives, as I note in Chapter 3. We received 236 responses. Of these 172 were trustees; the non-trustee component reflects the fact that several of the unions had no means of distinguishing trustees from all the members involved in pensions decision-making. The figures cited in the text are from a base total of 172, except where they are concerned only with bargaining, when the full sample is used. (See p. 70 for a discussion of the term 'member trustee').

The pensions manager and member trustee surveys were designed to run in parallel as far as possible, with overlapping questions, but not rigidly so.

(3) *Case studies* of 18 public- and private-sector organisations. These were selected to cover a range of sizes, industrial sectors and geographical locations. The case studies were based on semi-structured interviews, usually lasting about one and a half hours, with a variety of people selected according to the character of the scheme's management structure: member and management trustees; pensions negotiators from both sides; pensions, personnel and finance managers; and other participants such as management committee members. We conducted a total of 126 interviews. On the whole, the case studies were of organisations at the forefront of pensions policy and participation. Co-operation with access and information (which we had in large measure) is inevitably more forthcoming from organisations with a concern for pensions and confidence in their own practices.

(4) Within 11 of the case study organisations, we surveyed a sample of *scheme members*. This survey dealt with the information they

received and their perceptions of participation. I have not drawn on this data in the text; for details see Hyman and Schuller, 1983.

(5) A postal survey of *union headquarters*. This survey dealt with the services unions provide for their representatives, including trustees and negotiators. We received responses from 20 unions.

References

Andrew, E. *Closing The Iron Cage: the scientific management of work and leisure*, Black Rose Books, Quebec. (1981)

Andrews-Jones, D. and Churchill, J. 'Consultative and negotiating arrangements' in *Pensions – Involving the Members*, Institute of Personnel Management, London. (1983)

Artus, R. and Minto, G. 'The financial and economic role of pension funds' in *Pension Funds and Their Advisers 1984*, AP Information Services, London. (1984)

Bagehot, W. *Lombard Street*, Smith, Elder, London. (1912)

Baldamus, G. *Efficiency and Effort: An Analysis of Industrial Administration*, Tavistock, London. (1961)

Baldwin, S. *Pension Funds and Ethical Investment*, Council on Economic Priorities, Washington, DC. (1980)

Barber, Randy, 'Pension Funds in the United States: issues of investment and control', *Economic and Industrial Democracy* 3:1. (1982).

Batchelor, C. 'Competing institutions and their approaches', *Financial Times*, February 12. (1984)

Batstone, Eric, *Industrial Democracy: European Experience*, HMSO, London. (1976)

Batstone, Eric, *Working Order: Industrial Relations over Two Decades*, Blackwells, Oxford. (1984)

Batstone, Eric, Ferner, Anthony and Terry, Michael, *Unions on the Board*, Blackwells, Oxford. (1983)

Berle, A. *Property Without Power*, Harcourt Brace, New York. (1959)

Berle, A. and Means, G. *The Modern Corporation and Private Property*, Macmillan, New York. (1932)

BIM *Company Pension Schemes Survey*, British Institute of Management, London. (1984)

Blackburn, R. 'The new capitalism' in R. Blackburn (ed.) *Ideology in Social Science*, Pelican, London. (1972)

Blasi, J., Mehrling, P. and White, W.F. 'The politics of worker ownership in the US' in C. Crouch and F. Heller (eds.) *International Yearbook of Organizational Democracy Vol. I: Organizational Democracy and Political Processes*, John Wiley, London. (1983)

Blumberg, Paul, *Industrial Democracy: The Sociology of Participation*, Constable, London. (1968)

Brannen, P., Batstone, E., Fatchett, D. and White, P. *The Worker Directors*, Hutchinson, London. (1976)

Braverman, H. *Labor and Monopoly Capital*, Monthly Review Press, New York. (1974)

Bristow, Edward, 'Profit-sharing, socialism and labour unrest' in K.D. Brown (ed.) *Essays in Anti-Labour History*, Macmillan, London. (1974).

Brittan, S. *Jobs, Pay, Unions and the Ownership of Capital*, Financial Times (1984).

Brookes, C. *Boards of Directors in British Industry*, Department of Employment Research Paper No. 12, London. (1979).

Brown, W. *The Changing Contours of Industrial Relations in Great Britain*, Blackwells, Oxford. (1981).

Bullock Report, *Industrial Democracy*, Cmnd 6706, HMSO, London. (1977).

Carnegie, A. *The Gospel of Wealth*, New York. (1900).

Casey, Bernard and Bruche, Gert, *Work or Retirement?*, Gower, Aldershot. (1983).

CBI, *Current Employee Involvement Practice in British Business*, Confederation of British Industry, London. (1981).

CIR, *Industrial Relations in Multi-plant Undertakings*, Commission for Industrial Relations, Report 85, HMSO, London. (1974).

Clarke, Tom, *Contrasting Theories of Cooperative Production*, Discussion Paper 7, Centre for Research in Industrial Democracy and Participation, Glasgow University. (1983).

Clegg, H. *The System of Industrial Relations in Great Britain*, Blackwells, Oxford. (1979).

Clegg, H. *A New Approach to Industrial Democracy*, Blackwells, Oxford. (1960).

Coakley, J. and Harris, L. *The City of Capital*, Blackwells, Oxford. (1983).

Coates, Ken, *The New Worker Cooperatives*, Spokesman Books, Nottingham. (1976)

Coates, K. and Topham, T. *The New Unionism*, Penguin, London. (1974).

Cole, K. 'Member participation', *Pensions World* **10**:7. (1981).

Coopers & Lybrand, *The Management and Reporting of Pension Funds*, London. (1982).

Cressey, P., Eldridge, J., MacInnes, J. and Norris, G. *Industrial Democracy and Participation: A Scottish Survey*, Department of Employment Research Paper 28, London. (1981).

Crosland, C.A.R. *The Conservative Enemy*, Cape, London. (1962).

Crossman, R.H.S. *The Politics of Pensions*, Eleanor Rathbone Memorial Lecture, Liverpool University Press. (1972).
Crouch, Colin, *Trade Unions: The Logic of Collective Action*, Fontana, London. (1982).
Cubbin, John and Leech, Dennis, 'The effect of shareholding dispersion on the degree of control in British companies: theory and measurement', *Economic Journal* 93. (1983).
Culverhouse, Alan, 'Pensions in perspective', *Personnel Executive*, April. (1982).
Daniel, W. and Millward, N. *Workplace Industrial Relations in Britain*, Heinemann, London. (1983).
Davies, Paul and Lord Wedderburn of Charlton, 'The Law of Industrial Democracy', *Industrial Law Journal* 6:3. (1977).
De Vroey, M. 'The corporation and the labor process: the separation of ownership and control in large corporations', *Review of Radical Political Economics* 7:2. (1975).
DHSS, *Greater Security for the Rights and Expectations of Members of Occupational Pension Schemes*, Department of Health and Social Security, London. (1984).
DHSS, *Reform of Social Security: Programme for Change*, Vol. 2, Cmnd 9518. (1985).
Dobie, Claire, 'The smash and grab pension raiders', *Investors' Chronicle*, 15 February. (1985).
Drucker, Peter, 'Pension fund "socialism"', *Public Interest* 42. (1976).
EEC, *Employee Participation and Company Structure*, Brussels. (1975).
Elliott, John, *Conflict or Cooperation? The Growth of Industrial Democracy*, Kogan Page, London. (1978).
Ellison, Robin, *Private Occupational Pension Schemes*, Oyez Press, London. (1979).
Espinosa, Juan and Zimbalist, Andrew, *Economic Democracy: Workers' Participation in Chilean Industry 1970-73*, Academic Press, New York. (1978).
ETUI, *Trade Unions and Collective Capital Formation*, European Trade Union Institute, Brussels. (1983).
Fanning, D. *'Pension funding: the urgent need for change'*, *Journal of General Management* 7:3. (1983).
Francis, A. 'Families, firms and finance capital', *Sociology* 14:1. (1980).
GAD, *Occupational Pension Schemes 1979: Sixth Survey*, Government Actuary's Department, HMSO, London. (1981).
Gaullier, Xavier, *L'Avenir à reculons: chomage et retraite*, Editions Ouvrieres, Paris. (1982).
Giddens, Anthony, *Central Problems in Social Theory*, Macmillan, London. (1979).
Gorz, André, *Pathways to Paradise*, Pluto Press, London. (1985).

Green, Francis, 'Occupational pension schemes and British capitalism', *Cambridge Journal of Economics* 6. (1982).

Guillemaud, Anne-Marie, 'Jalons pour une sociologie des politiques sociales: le cas de la politique française de la vieillesse', *Sociologie et Sociétés* 16:2. (1984).

Haber, C. 'Mandatory retirement in 19th Century America' *Journal of Social History* 12:1. (1978).

Haberman, Steven, 'Future Dependency' in City University Centre for Research in Insurance and Investment, *Pensions: The Problems of Today and Tomorrow*, Institute of Actuaries, London. (1985).

Hager, D. quoted in 'Fund Managers Survey', *Pensions* 4:1 (1982).

Hannah, Leslie, *The Rise of the Corporate Economy* (1st edn), Methuen, London. (1976).

Hannah, Leslie, *Terms and Conditions of Early Pension Schemes*, Business History Unit, Pensions Working Paper 3, London School of Economics. (1983).

Hannah, Leslie, *Inventing Retirement*, Cambridge University Press. (1986).

Hills, John, *Savings and Fiscal Privilege*, Institute of Fiscal Studies, London. (1984).

Hirschman, A. *Exit, Voice and Loyalty*, Harvard University Press. (1970).

Horvat, Branko, *The Political Economy of Socialism*, Martin Robertson, Oxford. (1982).

Hyman, Jeff and Schuller, Tom, *Employee Participation in the Management of Pension Schemes'*, Centre for Research in Industrial Democracy and Participation, Glasgow University. (1983).

Hyman, Jeff and Schuller, Tom, 'Occupational pension schemes and collective bargaining', *British Journal of Industrial Relations* 22:3. (1984).

IDE, *Industrial Democracy in Europe*, Oxford University Press. (1981).

IDS, *Profit Sharing and Share Options*, Incomes Data Services Study 306, London. (1984).

Ingham, Geoffrey, *Capitalism Divided?*, Macmillan, London. (1984).

IRRR, 'Member participation in pension schemes', *Industrial Relations Review and Report* 251. (1981)

James, S. 'The role of the external adviser', *Pensions World* 12:8 (1983).

Jones, D. 'Producer cooperatives in industrialized Western economies', *British Journal of Industrial Relations* 18:2. (1980).

Knightley, Philip, *The Vestey Affair*, Macdonald Futura, London. (1981).

Labour Party Study Group, *Capital and Equality* (Opposition Green Paper), Labour Party, London. (1973).

Lascelles, D. 'Warburg sets out blueprint for a financial wonder

machine', *Financial Times*, February 22. (1985).
Liberal Industrial Inquiry, *Britain's Industrial Future*, Benn, London. (1928).
Linton, Martin, *The Swedish Road to Socialism*, Fabian Tract 503, London. (1985).
Litvak, L. *Pension Funds and Economic Renewal*, Council of State Planning Agencies, Washington, DC. (1981).
Locksley, Gareth and Minns, Richard, 'Pension power', *Marxism Today*, August. (1984).
Longstreth, F. 'The City, industry and state' in C. Crouch (ed.) *State and Economy in Contemporary Capitalism*, Croom Helm, London. (1979).
Lynes, Tony, 'Pensions in secret', *New Society* 329. (1969).
Lyon, Stewart. 'The outlook for pensioning', *Journal of the Institute of Actuaries*, 110:1. (1983).
McGoldrick, Ann. *Equal Treatment in Occupational Pension Schemes*, Equal Opportunities Commission, Manchester. (1984).
Malca, E. *Pension Funds and Other Institutional Investors*, D.C. Heath, (1975).
Malcolm, David. 'Investment by pension funds – an assessment of quality', Financial Times conference on *Pensions in 1985*, 23 January. (1985).
Manly, H.W. 'On the valuation of staff pension funds', *Journal of the Institute of Actuaries* 36. (1901).
Mares, Judith, *The Use of Pension Fund Capital: Its Social and Economic Implications*, President's Commission on Pension Policy, Washington, DC. (1979).
Marsden, David, *Industrial Democracy and Industrial Control in West Germany, France and Great Britain*, Department of Employment Research Paper 4, London. (1978).
Marsh, A. *Employee Relations Policy and Decision Making*, Gower, Aldershot. (1982).
Meade, James, *Wage Fixing*, Allen & Unwin, London. (1982).
Melling, J. 'Employees, industrial welfare and the struggle for workplace control in British industry 1890:1920' in H. Gospel and C. Littler (eds.) *Managerial Strategies and Industrial Relations*, Heinemann, London. (1983).
Miller, Michael, *The Bon Marché*, Princeton University Press, New Jersey. (1981).
Minns, Richard, *Pension Funds and British Capitalism*, Heinemann, London. (1980).
Moher, J. *Trade Unions and Occupational Pension Schemes*, Pensions Management Institute, London. (1979).
NAPF, *Member Participation in Pension Schemes: A Guide to Good Practice*,

National Association of Pension Funds, Surrey. (1982).
Nichols, T. *Ownership, Control and Ideology*, Allen & Unwin, London. (1969).
Nobles, Richard, 'Conflicts of interest in trustees' management of pension funds: an analysis of the legal framework', *Industrial Law Journal* 14:1. (1985).
Norton-Taylor, Richard, *Whose Land Is It Anyway?*, Turnstone Press, Wellingborough. (1982).
Nyman, S. and Silberston, A. 'The ownership and control of industry', *Oxford Economic Papers* 30:1. (1978).
OPB, *Greater Security for the Rights and Expectations of Members of Occupational Pension Schemes*, Cmnd 8649, HMSO, London. (1982).
OPB, *Improved Protection for the Occupational Pension Rights and Expectations of Early Leavers*, Cmnd 8271, HMSO, London. (1981).
OPB, *Solvency, Disclosure of Information and Member Participation in Occupational Pension Schemes*. Occupational Pensions Board, Cmnd 5904, HMSO (3 vols). (1975).
Orwell, George, *Animal Farm*, Secker & Warburg, London. (1945).
Pahl, R.E. *Divisions of Labour*, Blackwells, Oxford. (1984).
Pahl, R. and Winkler, J. 'The economic elite: theory and practice' in P. Stanworth and A. Giddens (eds.) *Elites and Power in British Society*, Cambridge University Press. (1974).
Pateman, Carole, *Participation and Democratic Theory*, Cambridge University Press. (1970).
Phillipson, Chris, *Capitalism and The Construction of Old Age*, Macmillan, London. (1983).
Piachaud, David, 'State pensions in Britain', *Journal of Social Policy* 12:2. (1983).
Pilch, M. and Wood, V. *Pension Schemes*, Gower, Aldershot. (1979).
Plender, John, *That's The Way The Money Goes*, André Deutsch, London. (1982).
Prais, S. *Productivity and Industrial Structure*, Cambridge University Press. (1982).
Purcell, Father Theodore, 'Thinking Ahead: public interest proxy resolutions exert influence on corporate decision-making', *Harvard Business Review*, Sept./Oct. (1979).
Ramsay, Harvie, 'Cycles of control', *Sociology* 11:3. (1977).
Reddin, M. 'Occupation, welfare and social division' in C. Jones and J. Stevenson (eds.) *Yearbook of Social Policy 1980–81*, Routledge and Kegan Paul, London. (1982).
Reid, Margaret, *The Secondary Banking Crisis 1973–75*, Macmillan, London. (1982).
Richardson, Lord, 'The provision of pensions', *Bank of England Quarterly Bulletin* 23:4. (1983).

Rifkin, Jeremy and Barber, Randy, *The North Will Rise Again: Pensions, Politics and Power in the 1980s*, Beacon Press, Boston. (1978).

Robertson, Don, 'How's it gawn, Jimmy?' in Tom Schuller (ed.) *Is Knowledge Power? Problems and Practice in Trade Union Education*, Aberdeen People's Press. (1981).

Rose, Harold, 'Occupational pension schemes – economic background and issues', *Bank of England Panel Paper 20*, London. (1983).

Rubinstein, W. 'Wealth, elites and class structure in Britain', *Past and Present* 6. (1977).

Ryan, Alan, *Property and Political Theory*, Blackwells, Oxford. (1984).

Salaman, G. 'Managing the frontiers of control' in A. Giddens and G. Mackenzie (eds.) *Social Class and the Division of Labour*, Cambridge University Press. (1982).

Saunders, Peter, 'Beyond housing classes: the sociological significance of private property rights and means of consumption', *International Journal of Urban and Regional Research* 8:2. (1984).

Schuller, Tom, 'The process of workforce polarization: occupation-based welfare and employee participation', *International Journal of Sociology and Social Policy* 4:1 (1984).

Schuller, Tom, *Democracy at Work*, Oxford University Press. (1985).

Scott, J. *Corporations, Classes and Capitalism*, Hutchinson, London. (1979).

Scott, J. 'Property and control' in A. Giddens and G. Mackenzie (eds.), *Social Class and the Division of Labour*, Cambridge University Press. (1982).

Slattery, P. 'The pension fund trustee – his role in law' in *Pension Fund Trusteeship in the 1980s*, CARL Communications, Middlesex. (1981).

Strinati, D. *Capitalism, The State and Industrial Relations*, Croom Helm, London. (1982).

Thane, Pat, 'The muddled history of retiring at 60 and 65', *New Society* 826. (1978).

Thomas, H. and Logan, C. *Mondragon: An Economic Analysis*, Allen & Unwin, London. (1982).

Thomas, Keith, 'Age and authority in early modern England', *Proceedings of the British Academy* 62. (1976).

Thompson, G. 'The firm as a 'dispersed' social agency', *Economy and Society* 11:3. (1982).

Thomson, A. and Beaumont, P. *Public Sector Bargaining*, Saxon House, Farnborough. (1978).

Thornley, Jenny, *Worker's Cooperatives: Jobs and Dreams*, Heinemann, London. (1981).

Titmuss, R. *The Irresponsible Society*, Fabian Tract 323, London. (1960).

Tomlinson, Jim, *The Unequal Struggle: British Socialism and the Capitalist Enterprise*, Methuen, London. (1982).

Towers, B., Chell, E. and Cox, D. *Worker Directors in Private Industry*, Department of Employment Research Paper 29, London. (1985).

TUC, *Takeovers, Mergers, Sell-offs*, Occupational Pensions Bulletin 9, Trades Union Congress, London. (1982).

TUC, *Member Trustees of Occupational Pension Schemes*, Trades Union Congress, London. (1984).

Useem, Michael, *The Inner Circle: Large Corporations and The Rise of Business Political Activity in the US and the UK*, Oxford University Press, New York. (1984).

Van Gunsteren, Herman and Rein, Martin, 'The Dialectic of Public and Private Pensions', *Journal of Social Policy* **14**:2. (1985).

Wall, T. and Lischeron, J. *Worker Participation*, McGraw Hill, London. (1977).

Ward, Sue, *Pensions*, Pluto Press, London. (1981).

Webb, S. and B, *A Constitution for the Socialist Commonwealth of Great Britain*, Longmans, London. (1921).

Weber, Arnold, 'Stability and change in the structure of collective bargaining' in Lloyd Ulman (ed.) *Challenges to Collective Bargaining*, Prentice Hall, Watford. (1967).

White Paper, *Occupational Pension Schemes: The Role of Members of the Running of Schemes*, Cmnd 6514, HMSO, London. (1976).

Whitley, R. 'The City and industry' in P. Stanworth and A. Giddens (eds.) *Elites and Power in British Society*, Cambridge University Press. (1974).

Wilson Committee, *Report of the Committee to Review the Functioning of Financial Institutions*, Cmnd 7937, HMSO, London. (1980).

Woodbury, S. 'Substitution between wage and nonwage benefits', *American Economic Review* **73**:1. (1983).

Index

accountability, 16, 59, 64-5, 102, 141, 152
  trustee, 74, 113, 127, 147-8
actuaries, 64, 132-3
  reports, 118, 119-20, 132-3
advisory personnel, 64, 108-12, 120-21
AFL-CIO, 102
age
  -dependency ratio, 5-6
  management of, 2, 5-11, 61, 66-7
  retirement (early), 8-10, 66, 75
  retirement (fixed), 24-5, 27, 76
agriculture, 13-14, 26
Andrews-Jones, D., 46
appointments (trustee function), 64, 108-12 *passim*, 120-21
Artus, R., 100
asset(s), 1-2, 50
  management, 11-16, 61-4, 108-9, 120-21, 124-9
  reversion, 49, 93
  see also capital; investment
Associated Communications Corporation, 99
Austria, 58

Bagehot, Walter, 152
Baldamus, G., 38
Baldwin, S., 100
banks, 17, 85-6, 87, 95, 98
  see also merchant banks
Barber, Randy, 11, 101
bargaining, 28, 33-5
  see also collective bargaining
Batchelor, C., 96
Batstone, Eric, 123, 134
benefit bargaining, 33-4
benefit levels, 2, 3, 4-6, 41, 44-50
Berle, Adolf, 11, 12, 82, 85
Bismarck, Otto von, 24-5, 27
Blackburn, R., 84
Blasi, J., 56
Blumberg, Paul, 17, 37
Brannen, P., 50, 130
Braverman, H., 27
Bristow, Edward, 55
Britain, 1-2, 8-9, 10
  pension fund assets, 11-16
British Business, 14
British Institute of Management, 117
British Rail, 1, 62, 99
British Steel Corporation, 21, 50, 130
British Telecom, 1
Brookes, C., 123
Brown, W., 44
Bruche, Gert, 9
Bullock Report, 37, 52, 67, 72, 141-2, 146-7, 154
  Minority Report, 18-19, 140

Caja Laboral Popular, 57
capital, 107, 143, 149-50
  control, 1, 3, 15, 80-86, 139-41
  disinvestment, 100-101
  industrial, 86, 87, 89-94
  investment, *see* investment

165

management of, 2, 11–16, 61, 66–7
ownership, *see* economic democracy
capitalism, 5, 81, 83–4, 100, 104, 149
case studies (Glasgow study), 46, 91, 111–12, 116–17, 121, 137, 141, 155–6
Casey, Bernard, 9
CBI survey, 45
Churchill, J., 46
CIR report, 51
Civil Service, 24, 25, 60
Clarke, Tom, 56
Clegg, Hugh, 37, 44
Coakley, J., 87, 98
Coates, Ken, 16, 56
Cole, K., 68, 78
collective bargaining, 17–20, 34
  in pensions, 38–53
  representation through, 33, 37–8
  see also industrial relations
Committee of Management, 60, 61
Companies Act (1980), 140, 143
company structure, 139–52
consultation, 16, 31–2, 45–50 *passim*
consultative committees, 20, 33, 73, 76
contract work, 19
contracting out, 25, 32, 48
contributory schemes, 31, 48, 70
control
  capital, 1, 3, 15, 80–86, 139–41
  in economic democracy, 3, 55–9
  institutional, 86–103
  ownership, 3, 12, 80–86, 88–97, 103
  welfare as, 27–30 *passim*, 36
Coopers and Lybrand, 47
Cressey, P., 45

Crosland, Anthony, 12, 83
Crouch, Colin, 41
Cubbin, John, 85
Culverhouse, Alan, 25

Daniel, W., 45, 52
decision-making, 37, 80
  expertise, 129–34
  participation, 16–71, 20, 21–2
  pensions, 20, 43, 48, 53, 114
  strategic, 139–49
  trustee, 72, 110, 112–13, 116
deferred pay concept, 3, 23, 28–35, 38–9, 42, 75–6, 139, 141
Denmark, 58, 77
deskilling, 27
De Vroey, M., 84
DHSS, 23
discretionary powers, 65–9, 90, 108–13 *passim*, 121, 136
disinvestment, 100–101
Dobie, Claire, 49
Donovan Report, 14
Drucker, Peter, 1–2, 11, 98

economic democracy, 3, 55–9
  industrial democracy and, 139–40
EEC, 20, 140
efficiency factor, 141, 144–5
Eldridge, J., 45
Elliot, B., 49
Elliott, John, 18
Ellison, Robin, 133
employee-employer relations, 3, 10, 23, 25, 27–31
employee participation, *see* participation
Employee Share Ownership Plans, 56
employers, 3, 10, 14, 23, 25, 27–31
  see also management
Employment Protection Act (1975), 18

Employment Protection (Consolidation) Act (1978), 66
Equal Opportunities Commission, 26, 46
equity capital, 1, 88–97 *passim*
ESOPs, 56
Ethical Investment Research and Information Service, 102
ETUI Report, 58
Evans v. London Co-op, 127–8
exchange controls, 14
external advisors, 89, 92, 93–6, 98

Fanning, D., 43
female workers, 5, 7–8, 24, 26, 143
final salary schemes, 30
Finance Act (1970), 66
financial expertise, 131–2
financial institutions
 control role, 85–6, 87–8
 as external advisers, 89, 93–7
 Wilson Committee, 6, 12, 15, 79
France, 8, 9, 58
Francis, A., 87
Friends Provident Stewardship Trust, 102, 103
functional rationale (participation), 141–4

Galbraith, J.K., 83
Gaullier, Xavier, 8
Germany, 10, 24–5, 58, 77, 146
Giddens, Anthony, 84
Gill, Jack, 99
Glasgow study, 3, 40, 41
 case studies, 46, 91, 111–12, 116, 121, 137, 141, 148, 155–6
 member trustee survey, 46, 48–50, 53, 60, 62, 69–71, 74, 108–21, 134–5, 155
 pensions manager survey, 10, 46, 48, 70–71, 73–4, 95, 98, 108–21, 154–5
 trade unions involved, 69–70, 155–6
Gomme Holdings, 49
government
 debt, 2, 13, 67, 80
 influence, 89, 93
 state pensions, 4, 21, 23–5
 see also local authorities
Government Actuary, 6, 7, 25–6, 45, 68–9, 70
gratuity concept, 23, 25, 27–30, 42, 141
Green, Francis, 30, 39
Green Paper (EEC), 140
Guillemaud, Anne-Marie, 9

Haberman, Steven, 6
Hager, D., 132
Hannah, Leslie, 27, 32, 133
Harris, L., 87, 98
health and safety, 20, 42, 48
Health and Safety at Work Act (1975), 18
Horvat, Branko, 37
House of Fraser, 97
Hyman, Jeff, 3, 44, 148, 156

IDE group, 16
IDS study, 55
incomes policy, 43, 44, 78
index-linking, 30, 39
industrial capital, 86, 87, 89–94
industrial democracy, 1, 2, 3, 139–40
 see also Bullock Report; collective bargaining; consultation; participation
industrial relations, 14, 44, 107 110, 113, 117
inflation, 12, 29, 30
information, 20, 49, 65–6
 dissemination, 3, 76–7, 108–14 *passim*, 117–20, 121

Ingham, Geoffrey, 86
Institute of Actuaries, 127, 137
institutional control, 86–103, 126
insurance companies, 11–13, 68, 85, 89, 93–4, 98, 119
interest groups, 150, 151
investment, 12, 15, 32–4, 35, 80, 90
  alternative strategies, 101–3
  information, 118, 119, 120
  legal obligations, 124–9
  overseas, 13, 14, 21, 62, 93, 125
  performance (monitoring), 61–2, 63, 108–13 *passim*, 121
  policy, 61–2, 108–13 *passim*, 115–16, 121, 123–5
  see also assets; investment managers
investment managers, 89, 91–2, 116, 120, 121
  external, 64, 94–7, 99–100
IRRR study, 45
Italy, 58

James, S., 133
Job Release Scheme, 9
Johnson Matthey Bank, 105
Joint Representation Committees, 52
Jones, D., 57
Jones, Jack, 19
Journal of the Institute of Actuaries, 30

Knightley, Philip, 23

labour market trends, 7–10
labour mobility, 28–9
land ownership, 13–14
  see also property
Lascelles, D., 98
Leech, Dennis, 85

legislation, 16, 19, 29, 38, 77–8, 147
  and legal obligations, 124–9
  trust law, 11, 32, 60, 124
legitimacy (of representatives), 38, 41, 146–8
Leverhulme Trust, 154
Liberal Industrial Inquiry, 82
Linton, Martin, 58
Lischeron, J., 16
Litvak, L., 11
local authorities, 12, 25, 60, 89, 93, 95, 103
Local Enterprise Boards, 93
Locksley, Gareth, 103
Logan, C., 57
Longstreth, F., 86
Lonrho, 97
Lynes, Tony, 32–3
Lyon, Stewart, 127

McGoldrick, Ann, 26, 46, 69
MacInnes, J., 45
Malca, E., 11
male workers, 7–8, 24
'managed fund', 68, 89, 94
management, 39, 44
  age, 2, 5–11, 61, 66–7
  appointments, 64, 108–12, 120–21
  asset, 11–16, 61–4, 108–9, 120–21, 124–9
  capital, 2, 11–16, 61, 66–7
  committees, 32, 60, 61, 68, 115
  democratisation, 2–3, 67–79
  external, 89, 92, 93–7
  internal, 89, 90–93, 94, 95
  ownership and, 81, 82–5, 90, 103
  structures, 33–5, 68, 75
Manly, H.W., 30–31
manual workers, 28–30, 32, 39–40, 46, 51–2, 72–3
Mares, Judith, 102
Marks and Spencers, 99

Marsh, A., 44
Marx, K., 81, 82
Meade, James, 146
Means, Gardiner, 11, 82, 85
Megarry, Sir Robert, 128
Mehrling, P., 56
Meidner, Rudolf, 58
member trustees, 38, 41, 151
  constraints, 15, 107, 121-36, 143
  contribution and effect, 110-21
  functions, 3, 108-10, 120-21, 141
  growth of, 3, 67-79
  influence, 3, 89-90, 115-16
  strategic participation, 139-49
  survey, 46, 48-50, 53, 60, 62, 69-71, 74, 108-21, 134-5, 155
merchant banks, 64, 93, 94, 95-7
Mercury International Group, 97-8
mergers, 17, 50, 52, 97
Mill, J.S., 115
Millward, N., 45, 52
miners' strike, 20, 36
Mineworkers' Pension Scheme case, 127, 128
Minns, Richard, 12, 94, 95, 98, 103
Minto, G., 100
Moher, J., 39
Mondragon co-operatives, 57
multi-level bargaining, 51-3
Murray, Len, 39
mutual funds, 11

National Association of Pension Funds, 36, 45, 66, 68, 74, 78, 105
National Coal Board, 1, 99, 128
National Insurance Act (1959), 25
National Pension Insurance Fund, 58-9
National Spinsters Association, 24
National Union of Mineworkers, 127-9
negotiations, 48-50
  see also collective bargaining; consultation
Neill, James, 49
Netherlands, 58, 77
Nichols, T., 85
non-contributory schemes, 31, 70
Norris, G., 45
Norton-Taylor, R., 14
Nyman, S., 85

occupational hierarchy (trustees), 72-3
occupational pension schemes, *see* pension funds; pensions
Occupational Pensions Board, 29, 65, 76-7, 93, 110, 117, 119, 137
Occupational Pension Schemes (White Paper), 67, 77-8
OECD countries, 5
overseas investment, 13, 14, 21, 62, 93, 125
ownership, 11, 12-16
  collective, 149-51
  in economic democracy, 3, 55-9
ownership control, 80-86, 103-4
  influence lines and, 88-97
  institutional control and, 86-103
Oxford study, 87

Pahl, R.E., 28
part-time work, 19, 26, 143
participation, 18-20, 28
  forms, 2, 16-17, 21-2, 30-35
  management structures and, 34-6
  strategic, 139-49

trustee, 69–71, 75–9, 107–37
Pateman, Carole, 16
pension funds, 5, 18, 49–50
  conflicting interests, 97–8
  control (institutional), 86–103
  control (ownership), 80–86, 103–4
  influence of, 88–97, 99–103
  legal obligations, 124–9
  social contracts and, 149–52
  strategic decision-making, 139–49
  see also asset(s); investment; pensions
Pension Reform Act (1974), (US), 11
pensions
  costs, 43–4
  decision-making, 20, 43, 48, 53, 114
  negotiations, *see* collective bargaining
  rule supervision, 64–5
  scheme evolution, 3, 23, 25–35
  state, 4, 21, 23–5
  transferability, 25, 28–9, 75, 102, 105
  see also deferred pay concept; gratuity concept
Pensions Investment Resource Centre, 103
pensions managers, 44, 66, 89, 90–91
  survey, 10, 46, 48, 70–71, 73–74, 95, 98, 108–21 *passim*
Phillipson, Chris, 8
Pilch, M., 43, 47, 92
Plender, John, 98, 125
Post Office, 1, 21, 99, 134
Prais, S., 86
private sector, 25, 26–7, 32, 68–9
privatisation, 40, 103
profit-maximisation, 83, 84, 104

profit-sharing schemes, 20, 55–6, 106
property, 12, 13–14, 60, 64, 80
  rights, 57, 59, 81–3, 141
provident funds, 36
Prudential Assurance, 99–100
public sector, 25, 26, 27, 32, 68–9
Purcell, Father Theodore, 101

quality circles, 17

railway companies, 27, 32
Ramsay, Harvie, 20
Rank Organisation, 99
Reddin, M., 38, 52
representation
  collective bargaining and, 33, 49–50
  legitimacy in, 38, 41, 146–8
  in pension management, 30–35
  trustee level, *see* member trustees
retirement
  trends, 2, 5–11
  see also age
Richardson, Lord, 15, 25
Rifkin, Jeremy, 11, 101
rights, 139–40, 151
  property, 57, 59, 81–3, 141
risk-taking, 124, 125–6, 128
Rose, Harold, 29
Rubinstein, W., 86
rule supervision, 64–5, 108–11, 121
Rules Clauses, 65
Ryan, Alan, 81

Salaman, G., 27
scheme members survey, 148, 155–6
Schuller, Tom, 16, 20, 42, 44, 55, 134, 146, 148, 156
Scott, J., 86
SERPS, 4, 21, 23–5

shareholders (power), 99–101, 126
shareholdings (distribution), 84–5, 88
Silberston, A., 85
Slater, Jim, 86
Slattery, P., 60
social class, 40, 149–52
social contracts, 4, 149–52
social management (of age), 7–8
Social Security Act (1973), 29, 33
Social Security Pensions Act (1975), 4, 31, 33, 44, 48, 77
socialism, 1–2, 82, 98
South Africa, 102, 105
Southwood Committee, 32
Spain, 57
state pensions, 4, 21, 23–5
Stevens, J.P., 101
stockbrokers, 64, 93, 94, 95, 96–7
Strinati, D., 52
subsidies, 9, 26, 150
superannuation, 32, 60
Superannuation Funds Office, 49, 66, 93
Sweden, 9, 58–9, 77
Switzerland, 77

takeovers, 17, 50, 52, 97
taxation, 26, 30–35, 143
temporary work, 26
TGWU, 19, 69, 155
Thane, Pat, 24
Thomas, H., 57
Thomas, Keith, 25
Thornley, Jenny, 56
Titmuss, Richard, 12, 27, 152
Tomlinson, Jim, 82
Topham, T., 16
Trade Union and Labour Relations Act (1974), 17–18
trade unions, 101, 102, 134, 146
  Donovan Report, 14
  employee participation and, 16–20
  in Glasgow study, 69–70, 155, 156
  member trustees and, 67, 73–4, 77–8, 135–6
  see also collective bargaining
training (member trustees), 134–6
transferability, 25, 28–9, 75, 102, 105
Trust Clauses, 65
trust deeds, 62, 64–5, 118
trust law, 11, 32, 60, 124
trustee boards, 1, 32, 34–5, 67
  composition, 68, 72–3, 75
  in economic democracy, 55–9
  participation, *see* member trustees; worker directors
  participation (strategic), 139–49
trusteeship, 59–67
trustees
  functions, 3, 15, 59–67, 108–10, 120–21, 141
  member, *see* member trustees
TUC, 19, 39, 102, 142
  guide, 63, 64, 65, 66, 137

unemployment, 6, 7–8, 9, 19, 38, 146
unit trusts, 105
United States, 1–2, 11
Unity Trust, 102
Useem, Michael, 85

venture capital, 116
Vesteys, 23
Volkswagen, 10

wage-earner fund, 58–9
wages, 19, 52
  see also deferred pay concept
Wall, T., 16
Warburg, 96, 97
Ward, Sue, 4
Watkinson, H., 28
wealth (distribution), 6, 11

Webb, S. and B.A., 57
Weber, Arnold, 51
welfare schemes, 27–30 *passim*, 36
White, W.F., 56
white collar workers, 28–30, 32, 39–40, 46, 52, 72–3
White Paper (1976), 18, 67
Wilson Committee, 6, 12, 15, 79
Wood, V., 43, 47, 92

worker directors, 21, 50, 130
   functionality and, 141–2, 143–4
   strategic participation, 139–49
   see also Bullock Report
workers' co-operatives, 56–7, 146
workers' control, 16, 107
Working Assets, 105
works councils, 146